An exhibition to mark the retirement of Sir Michael L
as Director of the National Gallery

The National Gallery, London
17 December 1986 to 15 February 1987

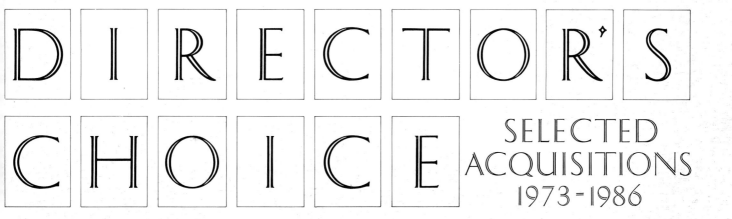

DIRECTOR'S
CHOICE SELECTED
ACQUISITIONS
1973-1986

Foreword

The number of outstanding paintings acquired for the National Gallery during Sir Michael Levey's directorship would be remarkable in any decade since its foundation, but seen in the context of the situation which confronted him when he became Director in 1973, the achievement is astonishing. The outlook then was bleak. Already through lack of funds and government indifference, that great masterpiece, the Velázquez *Juan de Pareja*, had been lost to the nation, leaving this country forever in 1970. In a period of economic decline and high taxation, a flood of sales by private individuals could be expected which, combined with the continued reluctance of the government to spend money on the arts, seemed bound to end in a major exodus of treasures. The apparatus of the Export Reviewing Committee provided a breathing space but no material support. In stark contrast to the situation here, the American, German and Japanese economies had prospered. Well-funded museums and wealthy individuals in those countries were ready and willing to pay spiralling prices to secure for themselves any major works of art they could from the diminishing pool left in private hands. Many of these works were still to be found in this country but their owners could be expected to sell under the steadily increasing financial pressures that confronted them.

It was against this bleak background that Sir Michael Levey and I first met in 1972 shortly before he became Director. Sir Michael was facing the first really important test since the loss of the Velázquez and trying to save Titian's great painting *The Death of Actaeon* from the same fate. Somehow the necessary funds were raised and I was to find my respect for Sir Michael still further increased. In addition to his knowledge, love and understanding of paintings he had revealed to me a strength of determination in their pursuit, whenever he judged it important for the National Gallery and the national interest.

In the decade that has followed his appointment, it is indeed remarkable that no great painting has escaped from these shores, certainly nothing approaching the importance of the Velázquez. Remarkable also is the number of masterpieces in this exhibition which, against all the odds, have been found and

secured for the National Gallery. It was not so surprising that in the nineteenth century Eastlake could visit Italy and return with great examples of the Italian School, or that the Trustees during Sir William Boxall's directorship could acquire seventy-seven pictures, including several Dutch masterpieces all from the heirs of Sir Robert Peel. In 1876 the Wynn Ellis bequest increased the Collection by no less than ninety-four paintings at a stroke. Such windfalls, alas, happen less frequently today. Nevertheless the Director has skilfully stretched our diminishing resources to make a series of acquisitions of the consistently high quality demanded by a great national collection and covering an immense range from Ugolino's *Moses* to Matisse's *Portrait of Greta Moll*. These acquisitions will remain a permanent memorial to his unerring eye, taste, expertise and the extraordinary range of his scholarship and interests.

Great collectors also need will-power, tenacity and courage. As for determination and tenacity, he has shown these qualities again and again, not least in his campaign to obtain the first painting by Jacques-Louis David to enter an English public collection. This was successful only after the most protracted and delicate negotiations, punctuated by periods of discouragement – the Trustees had virtually given up hope. His powers of persuasion were deployed to their utmost with the French Government and indeed the British, ending with this brilliant prize. His courage was displayed when he faced all the risks inherent in the recent acquisition of the Caravaggio. Not only was there the other version of the painting in the Fondazione Longhi, but there were also doubts about its condition. After cleaning, the quality of the painting more than justified the Director's confidence in his own judgement and the first secular painting by Caravaggio has triumphantly been added to the Collection.

Sir Michael has that rarest of qualities, essential to the great collector, a detachment from the day-to-day offerings of the market-place while remaining attuned to it. He will never fall into the trap that often ensnares the compulsive collector, who, in his acquisitiveness, develops a blind eye to the first-rate. Sir Michael stands back but remains alert, ready to descend on the real masterpieces without hesitation whenever they make an appearance. He has enriched our Collection by all the means available to a museum director – the David by agreement with the French Government, the Rubens *Samson and Delilah* through the auction rooms, the Fragonard from a dealer and works by Van Dyck, Claude, Poussin, Rembrandt and Drouais by negotiation and private treaty. Even when consciously he filled a 'gap' or added emphasis to an area of the Collection which had been weak in the past, as he did with the Meléndez, the first Spanish eighteenth century still-life to enter the Collection, or with the Drouais and Fragonard, both of which markedly strengthened the representation of the French eighteenth century paintings, the highest standards have been maintained.

We see clearly as a result of this exhibition that the acquisitions made during Sir Michael's directorship can more than hold their own against any other museum's collection made during this decade. They represent a fascinating and distinguished collection in themselves, and are, without exception, worthy also of the national collection which they now enhance. We as Trustees and all those in this country who love paintings will recognise now what we owe Sir Michael for his unswerving devotion, for his judgement and his knowledge which he has placed at the service of the National Gallery; we are deeply in his debt.

Jacob Rothschild
Chairman of Trustees, October 1986

Preface

To mark the retirement of Sir Michael Levey from the Directorship of the National Gallery, no event seemed more appropriate to his colleagues and to the Trustees than the present exhibition of Selected Acquisitions. The idea that he should present, within the limitations imposed by the Gallery's current Exhibition Room, those purchases that he most admired and should write about each of them was welcomed with characteristic enthusiasm by Sir Michael himself as a way of communicating to the public his own love of painting. The acquisition of these works for the nation to own and enjoy, sometimes achieved only after protracted and complex negotiations, is at the heart of the Gallery's existence and involves most if not all of the staff of the institution. But it is by no means its only function, and in most other ways the work of the Gallery has been transformed almost beyond recognition since the appointment of Sir Michael as Director in 1973.

Before any purchase is made by the Gallery, a report on the painting and its desirability for the Collection will be made to the Director by the member of the Keeper staff with responsibility for the relevant school of painting; the condition of the painting will be investigated by the Conservation Department. The

recommendation to pursue a major acquisition having been agreed by the Trustees, funds may not be immediately available from the Gallery's limited budget, even for a painting that has been offered for sale by private treaty under the beneficial terms of the 1976 Finance Act. Contributions towards the acquisition may have to be sought outside the building and the generosity of outside contributors, notably the National Heritage Memorial Fund, is manifest in the catalogue of the present exhibition.

Once secured for the Collection, a painting may require conservation work backed up by investigation by the Scientific Department; it may need reframing and careful consideration will have to be given to its location within the context of the Collection before preparations for the announcement of its acquisition can be made. A major purchase will transform the room where it eventually hangs, adding to the visitor's appreciation and understanding of the course of western painting and enhancing the works that are displayed nearby. It may suggest the theme for an exhibition, or be the subject of one of the series of Acquisition in Focus exhibitions that have taken place since 1982.

The acquisition of Velázquez's *The Immaculate*

Conception (No. 6424) which was purchased in 1974, was highlighted in the Exhibition 'The Working of the National Gallery', which marked the 150th anniversary of the founding of the Gallery in 1824. This was followed in 1974 by the first in a series of exhibitions, *Painting in Focus*, centered upon a single masterpiece – Holbein's *The Ambassadors* – which proved a great popular success and stimulated interest in mounting such exhibitions in other galleries and museums. In the following year space for the display of the permanent collection was greatly increased with the opening by H.M. the Queen of the Gallery's northern extension; the inaugural exhibition was one entitled *The Rival of Nature* which brought together Renaissance art in Italy with art of the same period from Northern Europe.

In rehanging the Collection after the opening of the Northern extension, efforts were made to provide a more sympathetic setting for the French 17th-century paintings with the loan of classical sculpture from the British Museum, and also for the earlier Italian paintings, with the introduction of more varied wall surfaces, creating niches for altarpieces, in some of the rooms where the ceilings had been sealed with lay-lights in the 1950s. Despite the provision of a small exhibitions gallery in the Northern extension, the lack of adequate space for larger exhibitions became fully apparent in 1976 with the mounting of *Art in 17th Century Holland*, the first of a series of large-scale loan exhibitions held at the Gallery. Catalogues of exhibitions – following the publication of the detailed catalogues of the Collection, inaugurated by Martin Davies and published in their final editions between 1957 and 1975 – have been the principal forum for scholarship within the building, together with the Gallery's Technical Bulletin, of which the first issue appeared in 1977.

The expansion of the Gallery's activities during Sir Michael's Directorship for the benefit of a wider public in London and beyond and for all age groups has been reflected in the initiatives of the Education Department and in the series of touring exhibitions, beginning with *Pictures from Eighteenth-Century Venice* (1976), which have been on display at several regional galleries during the course of a year. The interest of living artists in the Gallery's collection, however remote this is popularly imagined to be, has been brought into focus by the series of exhibitions, *The Artist's Eye*, in which a contemporary artist – beginning in 1977 with the sculptor Anthony Caro – chooses and brings together a group of paintings from the collection. Following on from this idea was the institution in 1980 of an artist-in-residence scheme, first undertaken by Maggi Hambling, whereby a distinguished younger painter works for a six-month period at the Gallery, exposed to the paintings on exhibition and to a regular dialogue with the public.

After the opening of the Northern Extension the main building work undertaken was the start of the air-conditioning scheme for the east wing of the Gallery, and the opening by the Prime Minister in 1980 of the first two rooms (41 and 43) forming part of this scheme. More attractive and spacious accommodation for the restaurant was at the same time provided on the ground floor beneath these rooms. The inauguration of the Sunley Exhibition Room in 1984 finally made possible – without disturbing the hanging of the permanent collection – the presentation of medium-sized exhibitions, like the one devoted to Danish painting which marked the opening of the room by Queen Margrethe of Denmark. Exhibitions that had preceded the opening of the Sunley Room included the series 'Second Sight' (1980-82), and the earliest of the Acquisition in Focus exhibitions. Beginning in 1978 a single painting lent from a regional gallery, and hung with the Gallery's collection, was the subject of the series 'A Month in London', and major loans from galleries abroad, exchanged with paintings borrowed for major exhibitions, have also been shown in this way.

Following this period of expansion and change under Sir Michael there came in 1985 the munificent gift of Mr J. Paul Getty junior and the consequent foundation of the American Friends of the National Gallery. In an otherwise inauspicious financial climate this gift has contributed significantly towards recent purchases, notably to the acquisition of Van Dyck's *'The Balbi Children'*, and to the restoration of the west wing dome and its four adjacent 'chapels' (Rooms 35-39) to their original richness of decoration. The expansion of the building on to the Hampton Site, for which earlier schemes for a partly commercial development had failed to win approval, was in the same year assured through the no less generous promise of Sir John Sainsbury, Mr Simon Sainsbury, and Mr Timothy Sainsbury MP, to fund an extension entirely for the use of the Gallery. Here the early Renaissance paintings of Italy and of Northern Europe will have a permanent home, and much-needed facilities, for lectures, for larger exhibitions, and for the sale of publications, will at last be provided.

The escalation of the Gallery's public activities in the past thirteen years, as this very brief résumé indicates, is unparalleled in the history of the institution; the range and quality of the paintings acquired has been comparably memorable, as the selection currently on exhibition clearly shows. Three further paintings would have been included in the exhibition, Giordano's *Perseus turning Phineas and his followers to stone*, Ter Brugghen's *The Concert*, and Købke's *Northern Drawbridge to the Citadel in Copenhagen*. The first is, however, too large in scale to be accommodated, the second had been promised as a loan abroad and the Købke, the first Danish painting to be purchased by the Gallery, has recently been put on show with the permanent Collection.

Very much a complement to the expansion of Gallery activities and to acquisition policy is the work represented by the bibliography of Sir Michael's principal writings on art, which follows the catalogue of the present exhibition: books and articles which cover virtually the whole range of Western European painting, not to mention sculpture, the art of Islam or civilisation more generally, and which transmit with his celebrated eloquence the author's abiding enthusiasm for works of art, and for 'Putting the art back into art history' – the subject of a paper that appeared in 1976. *Early Renaissance*, published in 1967, was the first book on art, as well as being the first paperback, to be awarded the Hawthornden prize; it was followed by *High Renaissance* in 1975. Scholarly articles that have appeared since 1953, usually several in a given year, have been backed up by the production of major catalogues. These have covered the Italian paintings of the 17th and 18th centuries in the National Gallery Collection (1956 and 1971) and the German paintings (1959), and the later Italian paintings in the Royal Collection (1964). There are more general books, to which many readers have gratefully owed their introduction to the pleasures of painting, *Giotto to Cézanne*, *Rococo to Revolution*, *Painting at Court*, and those devoted to more specialized aspects of Italian, French and German art, *Painting in 18th Century Venice, Art and Architecture of the 18th century in France, Dürer*.

Sir Michael's Gallery booklets have covered a range equally wide, from the first *Room to Room Guide* (1964), to booklets on Canaletto, Holbein, Hogarth, the Nude, the Venetian Scene, Ruisdael, and Velázquez and Murillo, and there have been the exhibitions on Gainsborough's *Daughters chasing a Butterfly*, Lawrence's portrait of Queen Charlotte, *The Neglected National Gallery*, and the monographic exhibition devoted to Lawrence at the National Portrait Gallery (1979). Happily 1986 and 1987 signal no abatement of this enjoyment in communicating the pleasure that works of art afford – there is shortly to appear an eagerly awaited monograph on the greatest Venetian painter of the 18th century, Giovanni Battista Tiepolo, and following that the volume on the 17th century in the Cambridge History of European Painting.

Allan Braham
Keeper and Deputy Director

Catalogue and bibliography

Note: the entries in the present catalogue are mainly based on information about the paintings supplied in National Gallery Reports (1973 to 1984). They have been compiled by Allan Braham, Alistair Smith, Christopher Brown, Michael Helston, and John Leighton, and in some cases derive from entries by Cecil Gould, Michael Wilson and Dillian Gordon.

Sir Michael's own views of the acquisitions are printed in italic after each catalogue entry.

The paintings are arranged and numbered in roughly chronological order. In the measurements height precedes width, and the size in metres is followed by that in inches.

The bibliography following the catalogue has been compiled by Allan Braham and John Leighton.

6484

6485

1-3   UGOLINO DI NERIO (active 1317-27)
Moses   (6484)

Poplar, 0.550 x 0.315 (21⅝ x 12⅜)
Purchased, 1983. Cleaned on acquisition
Inscribed, on Moses' scroll: Videbam que rubus aroebat
et non comburebatur (Exodus III:2); and, in the background: MOV/SES

David   (6485)

Poplar, 0.550 x 0.335 (21⅝ x 12⅜)
Purchased 1983. Cleaned on acquisition
Inscribed (much damaged) on David's scroll: De fructe
ventris tui ponam super sedem tuam (Psalms 131:11);
and, in the background, fragments of an identificatory
inscription

Two Angels   (6486)

Poplar, 0.270 x 0.560 (10½ x 22)
Purchased, 1983. Cleaned on acquisition
The angels are painted in the spandrels of an arch

The artist was also known as Ugolino of Siena and signed
himself as such on the high altarpiece of Santa Croce,
Florence. The above paintings and others in the Gallery
are satisfactorily identified as fragments of that altarpiece which was painted about 1325. Ugolino was
clearly a close follower of Duccio from whom he
derived several compositions.

The Santa Croce high altarpiece was commissioned by the Alamanni family. The inscription *Ugoli-
nus de Senis me pinxit* was still visible in the 18th
century on the central panel, a *Virgin and Child* (now
lost).

The altarpiece was dismantled in 1566 and fragments of it are consequently scattered throughout a
number of collections. In addition to these three
panels, the Gallery owns several others, namely: four of
the original seven predella panels (*The Betrayal of
Christ* [No. 1188], *The Ascent of Calvary* [No. 1189],
The Deposition [No. 3375], *The Resurrection* [No.
4191]); two fragments from the upper tier (*Saints
Simon and Thaddeus* [No. 3377] and *Saints Bartholomew and Andrew* [No. 3473]); a pair of angels
around an arch which originally framed a saint on the
main tier [No. 3378]; a pinnacle panel (*Isaiah* [No.
3376]). Other panels exist in Berlin, New York, Philadelphia and Los Angeles.

Moses and *David* would originally have formed
pinnacles and the pair of angels would have framed a
saint on the main tier. Much discussion has centred on
the reconstruction of the altarpiece. Dillian Gordon
and Anthony Reeve (*National Gallery Technical Bulletin*, Vol.8, London 1984) give an up-to-date summary
of the historical and technical evidence, and an account
of the conservation work undertaken. It is probable

6486

that all three panels formed part of the Young Ottley collection which was seen by Waagen in 1885. They were acquired by Herbert Cook in 1910 and purchased through Christie's by private treaty sale from the Trustees of the Doughty House Trust in 1983.

'It was a happy opportunity the Gallery was given – and gratefully took – in 1983 to add three more paintings to the group we already possessed from a major trecento *polyptych, painted by Ugolino for the high altar of S. Croce in Florence. Such paintings are not easy to show in a 19th century public building, and some people are perhaps shy of the non-naturalistic conventions of Ugolino's art. Yet a moment's pause over the* Moses *pinnacle alone reveals sinuous lines and delicate, leaf-green colour, enjoyable much as one enjoys an Islamic miniature – or a painting by Matisse.'*

---

4   THE MASTER OF THE BLESSED CLARE
(active mid 14th century)
The Vision of the Blessed Clare of Rimini   (6503)
Panel, 0.559 x 0.610 (22 x 24)
Purchased 1985.

A memorial, written in 1755, on the life of the Blessed Clare of Rimini describes two triptychs as having been on display on the church of San Francesco, Rimini. Each had *The Crucifixion* as central panel, *The Birth of Christ* on the left-wing and *The Vision of the Blessed Clare* on the right wing.

One of these triptychs remains intact in the Fesch Museum, Ajaccio. The left wing of the other is in the Lowe Art Museum, Miami; its *Crucifixion* is lost; the National Gallery painting was originally its right wing.

The Blessed Clare of Rimini was a Franciscan tertiary who died in 1326, and the painting is thought to have originated in the 1340s. The legend illustrated is portrayed extremely rarely. The *beata* kneels on the left. In her vision she received from Saint John the Evangelist a book decorated with golden letters. The saint had in turn received it from Christ, who, with the Apostles, shows the wounds in his hands and side.

The authorship of the two triptychs has been discussed by scholars with varying conclusions. Most recently they have been recognized as being by the

7

same hand, and the anonymous painter of both is described as The Master of the Blessed Clare, whose work exemplifies the unusual subject-matter and archaic style of a centre of production outside the main areas of development.

Known to be in the Ashburnham Collection in 1878, the painting was purchased in 1985 through Matthiesen Fine Art Ltd.

'The appeal of this early painting lies in its total pictorial clarity. Without needing to know precisely about the beata *and her vision, we can see a woman is kneeling to enjoy the company of sacred figures whose supernatural character is indicated by their giant stature. And although the panel was once part of a triptych, it admirably holds its own as a self-sufficient narrative scene.'*

5   THE MASTER OF THE SAINT BARTHOLOMEW ALTARPIECE
(active c.1470-c.1510)
The Virgin and Child with Musical Angels   (6499)

Oak, 0.520 x 0.380 (19½ x 15), round top
Inscribed: on the scroll held by the four angels above the Virgin's head, *regina celi letare* (Queen of Heaven rejoice)
Purchased 1985. Cleaned on acquisition

Bartholomew Altarpiece is now well represented in the Gallery, and he is a master of several moods. In this enchanting and original composition the mood is as joyous as a Christmas carol, positively infectious and almost slyly humorous.'

The Master is one of the most famous of anonymous artists, being the most accomplished and individual painter of the Cologne School around 1500. He is named from an altarpiece (Munich, Alte Pinakothek) originally painted for the church of Saint Columba in Cologne in the first years of the 16th century. It is now generally agreed that his activity spans the time from around 1470 to around 1510 and that he trained in the Netherlands, moving from a first base in Gelderland to Utrecht before travelling up the Rhine to Cologne where he became the outstanding artist of his time.

Scholars have dated this painting variously from 1480 to 1495, but it is nevertheless seen as a work of the Master's middle period. Technically it occupies a stage between the thinner, spontaneous application of the Master's youth (as exemplified in the Gallery's triptych attributed to the Master, No. 6497) and the layered, enamel-like surfaces of his mature work.

A small work doubtless made for private devotion in a domestic interior. The columbine in the left foreground is so-called because of its appearance (i.e. 'like a dove'), therefore makes symbolic allusion to the Holy Ghost. The painting was sold at Christie's in 1855, later entering the possession of the Christie-Miller family. It was acquired by private treaty sale through Sotheby's from Mr Andrew Christie-Miller, 1985.

'All too often the words 'German art' evoke the gloomy or the tortured – and not much help is given by free use of the term 'expressionist'. The Master of the S.

6   RAPHAEL (1483-1520)
Saint John the Baptist Preaching (6480)

Predella panel: area of painted surface 0.292 x 0.538 (top) and 0.528 (base) (11½ x 21³⁄₁₆ and 20¾)
Purchased, 1983. Cleaned and restored on acquisition

Saint John the Baptist Preaching, which had been on loan to the National Gallery since 1976, originally formed the left side of the predella panel of the *Ansidei Madonna* (No. 1171), which was acquired by the Gallery from the Marlborough collection at Blenheim Palace in 1885.

The altarpiece was painted by the young Raphael for the Ansidei chapel in the church of Saint Fiorenzo in Perugia, and it bears on the hem of the Madonna's robe a date which appears to be 1505. The predella was probably completed a little later, and it was originally decorated with three paintings: the Marriage of the Virgin (centre), a miracle of Saint Nicholas of Bari (right), and the Saint John the Baptist preaching (immediately below the figure of the saint in the main panel of the altarpiece). The first two scenes, which may have been in poor condition, have not been traced since the middle years of the 18th century, when the interior of Saint Fiorenzo was redecorated, and the altarpiece dismembered and sold.

No. 6480 had become much darkened with accumulations of dirt and discoloured varnish, and its restoration upon acquisition revealed the full brilliance of the painter's colouring and the subtlety of the handling, notably in the treatment of each individual figure and face. Colour and characterisation play their part in the ingenious treatment of the narrative, illustrating the theme of preaching, and related to more celebrated compositions that Raphael later created in the Vatican *stanze* and in the Tapestry cartoons. The original setting of the altarpiece and the restoration of No. 6480 are discussed by Allan Braham and Martin Wyld in the *National Gallery Technical Bulletin*, vol 8, 1984, pp. 15-23.

The Ansidei altarpiece and the *Saint John the Baptist Preaching* were acquired in Italy, in the 1760s, by Lord Robert Spencer, a younger son of the 3rd Duke of Marlborough. After his return he presented the altarpiece to his brother, the 4th Duke, retaining the predella panel until 1799 (Lord Robert Spencer sale, Christie's, 31st May, lot 86). It passed in the early years of the 19th century to the Lansdowne collection and was purchased through Messrs Christie by private treaty sale in 1983.

' I often think that Italian Renaissance painters may have found relief – as sometimes do spectators today – in turning from the large-scale altarpiece to the predella below it. The cool gravity of the main panel of the Ansidei Madonna *is certainly complemented by the surviving portion of its predella, which shows Raphael's vivacity as a story-teller and his keen eye for varied ages and physiognomies in the crowd assembled to hear the Baptist preach. '*

6451

6452

7-8 PONTORMO (1494-1557)
Joseph sold to Potiphar (6451)

Panel, 0.610 x 0.516 (24 x 20⁵⁄₁₆); painted surface, within a brown painted border, 0.590 x 0.506 (23¼ x 19¹⁵⁄₁₆)

Pharaoh with his butler and his baker (6452)

Panel, 0.610 x 0.517 (24 x 20³⁄₈); painted surface, within a brown painted border 0.597 x 0.510 (23½ x 20⅛)

Both purchased 1979, and cleaned on acquisition

These two paintings, together with No. 6453 (*Joseph's brothers beg for help (The Triumph of Joseph)*, which was acquired at the same time, formed part of a scheme of bedroom decoration carried out by Andrea del Sarto, Francesco Granacci, Pontormo and Bacchiacca in the Palazzo Borgherini in Florence on the occasion of the wedding in 1515 of Pierfrancesco Borgherini and Margherita Accaiuoli. The decoration, which is mentioned on several occasions in Vasari's *Lives*, consisted of panelling, *cassoni*, chairs and a marriage bed with inset paintings illustrating the story of Joseph. Three other panels from the same scheme of decoration were acquired by the National Gallery in the 19th century: the larger Pontormo, No. 1131, *Joseph with Jacob in Egypt*, and two by Bacchiacca, Nos. 1218 and 1219, *Joseph receives his brothers on their return to Egypt* and *Joseph forgives his brothers.*

In addition to the six panels in the National Gallery, nine other paintings almost certainly from the same scheme are known, in the Pitti and Uffizi Galleries in Florence (by Sarto and Granacci), in the Borghese Gallery in Rome (by Bacchiacca) and at Berlin (a circular painting of the Trinity, also by Granacci). Thanks largely to the liveliness of Pontormo's contributions to the series, the scheme of decoration became one of the most famous works of early 16th-century art in Florence, and, according to Vasari, during the brief Republic of 1529-30 an attempt was made by the Florentine government to confiscate the paintings and present them to their ally, King Francis I of France.

Fourteen of the panels illustrate scenes from the story of Joseph, and Nos. 6541 and 6542, which appear to be the second and the fourth of the fourteen in chronological order, probably decorated the panelling above the bed. No. 6453, apparently the sixth in the series, probably decorated the front of a chest (*cassone*).

The inscriptions on No. 6453, referring to Joseph as Christ's precursor as *Saviour of the World*, which seem surprising in the context of a bedroom, underline the parallel that was commonly drawn between the story of Joseph and the life of Christ, in this case with the miracle of the loaves and the fishes. Nos. 6451 and 6452 illustrate incidents otherwise very rarely shown in art, and the equivalent incidents from the New Testament are the betrayal of Christ and the story of the good and bad thieves. The reconstruction of the series and the significance of the themes is further discussed by Allan Braham in *The Burlington Magazine*, December 1979, pp.754-65.

The three panels formed part of the Cowper collection at Panshanger, Hertfordshire, for which most of the Italian paintings were acquired during the long residence in Florence of Henry Nassau, 3rd Earl Cowper (died 1789). Since 1970 they had been exhibited on loan at the National Gallery.

Acquired through Christie's, with the aid of a contribution from the National Art-Collections Fund (Eugene Cremetti Fund), 1979.

'It was in 1882 that the Gallery bought its first Pontormo, Joseph with Jacob in Egypt — a brave buy at the period, when the painter was quite out of fashion, and a beautiful work of art. Nearly a century later, we were able to add three more paintings by the artist from the same decorative series, helping to extend awareness, I hope, of his profound originality and stunning, ever-idiosyncratic colour schemes.'

---

9 PARMIGIANINO (1503-1540)
The Mystic Marriage of S. Catherine (6427)
Panel, 0.742 x 0.572 (29³⁄₁₆ x 22½)
Purchased, 1974. Cleaned on acquisition

The only work by Parmigianino which the Gallery had previously acquired was the big altarpiece of the Madonna and Child with the Baptist and S. Jerome (No. 33) dating from the artist's Roman period (1524-27) which was presented in 1826. The present picture complements it well, being smaller and more intimate. It may also date from the Roman period or from a little later when Parmigianino was resident in Bologna (1527-31). It is of strikingly brilliant execution and, since cleaning at the Gallery, revealed as in excellent condition. The painting was first published by Sydney J. Freedberg, *Parmigianino*. 1950, pp.172-75; it is further discussed by Cecil Gould in National Gallery Catalogues, *The Sixteenth-Century Italian Schools*, 1975, addendum, and in the the *Burlington Magazine*, April 1975, pp.230-33, where the sources of the composition in the work of Correggio, Michelangelo, and Raphael are analysed.

The picture was in the Borghese collection in Rome in the 17th and 18th centuries, was imported into England by W.Y. Ottley during the Napoleonic period and belonged to the Earls of Normanton from 1832. It was exhibited in London in 1959 (Agnew's, no. 65) and 1960 (Royal Academy, no. 97), and at Manchester in 1965 (no. 178). In the Countess of Normanton sale, Christie's, 29 November 1974 (lot 40), bought in. Purchased subsequently from the Countess of Normanton by the Gallery.

'The National Gallery cannot, unfortunately, display Parmigianino as a draughtsman but this small-scale painting is handled with much of the felicity of

his drawings, sketched in pigment with a sophisticated accomplishment paralleled by the inventiveness of the composition. The graceful main figure-group is placed between the bold foreground profile and that mysterious inner room in the distance, an unexpected, perpetually intriguing vista.'

10 PARMIGIANINO (1503-40)
Portrait of a Man (6441)

Panel, 0.890 x 0.640 (35¼ x 25⅛)
Purchased, 1977. Cleaned on acquisition

collector. The sitter holds what is probably a book in a jewelled binding; classical coins and a statuette lie on the table, and the relief to the left probably represents Venus and Mars with Cupid.

The style of the picture suggests that it was executed just before Parmigianino's journey to Rome, which probably took place in 1524. It is recorded as a portrait of a priest in the Farnese Collection at Parma at an early date (demonstrably within the seventeenth century, and probably before 1600) and was then transferred to Naples with the other Farnese works of art in the mid-eighteenth century. As a result of the Napoleonic invasion of Italy it changed hands, and is recorded in the possession of William Young Ottley by 1801. It was acquired by an ancestor of the late owner at Lord Radstock's sale in 1826. The picture, having previously been on loan to the Gallery, was sold by the Trustees of the Wrotham Park Picture Settlement at Christie's, 8 July 1977 (lot 117) and purchased by Sir Geoffrey Agnew, acting on behalf of the National Gallery.

‘ Rarity and intensity meet in this almost balefully memorable portrait, stamped with all Parmigianino's highly-strung individuality. If it dates from as early as 1524, it is the more extraordinary as the work of an artist aged only twenty-one. The setting is at least as haunting as the sitter, with its strange strip of landscape and exquisitely elegant bas-relief, classical in subject-matter yet surely chiselled out of Parmigianino's own imagination. ’

Parmigianino was one of the most enterprising portrait painters of his time in Italy, when portraits were expanding from head-and-shoulders to half length, and could thus include some of the sitter's possessions. Before the acquisition of No. 6441 the Gallery had no example of Parmigianino's portraiture, and there is only one other generally admitted in the British Isles (in the Royal Collection at Hampton Court).

The sitter of the present portrait is not identified. He has been thought to be Francesco Baiardo, who was a patron of the artist in Parma, and known to be a

11 JACOPO BASSANO
(active c.1535; died 1592)
The Way to Calvary   (6490)
Canvas, 1.450 x 1.330 (57 x 52½)
Purchased, 1984.

The Way to Calvary is one of the most famous works of the Venetian-trained artist Jacopo da Ponte (the son of a local painter active in the town of Bassano in the Veneto). Painted probably about 1540, *The Way to Calvary* is one of a group of canvases which show a sudden widening of Bassano's art before the appearance of the more specialised works of his later years, particularly rustic subjects and night scenes, which continued to be popularised by the studio of the painter under the direction of one or other of his four sons until the end of the 16th century.

For this particular subject, Bassano adopts a densely crowded design of the kind more familiar in central Italian painting in the mid-16th century. To this is added an intensity of colouring characteristic of the Venetian tradition - most closely paralleled in the earliest works of Veronese — and a psychological expressiveness that recalls the work of Dürer and other north European artists. The painting joins two others by Bassano in the National Gallery collection, a small composition of *The Good Samaritan* (No. 277) and a much later painting of *The Purification of the Temple* (No. 228).

The painting was shown in the Royal Academy *The Genius of Venice* exhibition, 1983, no. 4.

It is of considerable 'heritage' interest since it was one, bearing an attribution to Veronese, of the group of Italian paintings given by the States of Holland to King Charles II on his accession to the throne of England in 1660. By the 1720s it was in the possession of Lord Torrington and it passed by family descent to the Earls of Bradford at Weston Park. The acquisition was negotiated, through Christie's, as a private treaty sale from the Trustees of the Earl of Bradford, and with the aid of a generous contribution from the National Heritage Memorial Fund in 1984.

⟨ We probably have Charles I to thank for England's long tradition of liking the work of Bassano, and it seems apt that this Bassano should have been among the paintings presented by the States General to his son Charles II at the Restoration. Bassano is a master of inelegance, forceful and unafraid here to depict S. Veronica, dressed not in timeless robes but contem-

porary costume, awkwardly on her knees and almost clumsily thrusting out her cloth towards the suffering Christ, in an agony of compassion and anxiety. ⟩

12 ALBRECHT ALTDORFER
(born shortly before 1480, died 1538)
Christ taking Leave of his Mother (6463)

Limewood, 1.410 x 1.110 (55 x 43½)
Inscribed: 520 (for the date 1520) on the column
above the women
Purchased 1980. Cleaned on acquisition

Altdorfer was one of the principal exponents of land-scape painting in 16th-century Germany and central to the development of the so-called 'Danube School'. He became a citizen of Regensburg in 1505 and was resident there for much of his life. His formative travels were probably eastwards along the Danube. In 1519 he became a member of the Outer Council of Regensburg and was immediately involved in the expulsion of the town's Jewish community to whom most of the Christian merchants were in debt, going with other councillors to the Jewish quarter to read the edict of expulsion. This was carried out with the cruelty characteristic of the time.

When painting his *Christ taking Leave of his Mother* a year later, Altdorfer must have brought to mind the break-up of Jewish families, setting the event outside a town gate. Despite his anti-Semitism, he treats all parties with great sympathy.

The subject is rare in art before the early 16th century, although it then became quickly popular, particularly in Southern Germany. It is not included in the New Testament but appears almost simultaneously in two independent texts written in the early 14th century − one, the so-called 'Pseudo-Bonaventura', a text of *Meditations on the Life of Christ* composed by Fra Johannes de Caulibus in N.W. Italy; the other is the Middle High German *Marienleben* of Brother Philipp the Carthusian. By the time Altdorfer came to make his painting, the scene formed part of the passion plays popular at the time. In that performed in nearby Augsburg, Christ says farewell to his mother on three different occasions, which surely documents the thirst of the late medieval audience for scenes of pathos. In the painting, the prostrate Virgin is accompanied by Maria Cleophas, Maria Salome and Maria Jacobi. We are able to identify the woman in blue (from the Augsburg Passion Play's stage directions) as the Magdalen. On the right, Altdorfer develops a contrast between the aged, stooping Saint Peter and the youthful Saint John the Evangelist. In the background is the man whom Peter and John will meet and who will prepare the Last Supper.

The earliest reference to the painting dates only from 1809. At that time it was seen by Halm (forenames unknown) who recorded the collection of the Prince Abbot of St. Emmeram in Regensburg. He described it as the *Epitaph of a Family of Regensburg Citizens.* Unfortunately, the donor's family (bottom right) is not identified. Halm also described the painting as being signed with the artist's monogram and dated 1522. Neither of these inscriptions is now visible. (For some comment, see Alistair Smith in the *National Gallery Technical Bulletin*, vol. 7, 1983.) The first English owner was the Rev. John Fuller Russell, collector, theologian and author, who had a number of old paintings, mainly of the Italian School, some of which are now in the National Gallery. Sold, after his death, at Christie's on 18 April 1885 for twenty-three guineas, it passed through the hands of R. Langton Douglas before being acquired by Sir Julius Wernher in 1904. For some years on exhibition at Luton Hoo, as well as being on loan at the National Gallery (1945-49), Wildenstein, London (1946) and Manchester (1957). Acquired by private treaty sale, through Christie's, from the Wernher Estates in 1980, with the aid of generous contributions from the National Heritage Memorial Fund, the Pilgrim Trust and the National Art-Collections Fund (Eugene Cremetti Fund).

For a fuller account of the painting see Alistair Smith: *Christ taking Leave of His Mother*: Acquisition in Focus exhibition booklet, London, 1983/4.

‹ It is sad that there is no modern book in English on Altdorfer − sad and perhaps significant. Were he an Italian artist, everyone would have heard about and praised Altdorfer. This great painting by him can be enjoyed for, if nothing else, its tremendous landscape, with a strong sense of crystalline, blue, Alpine atmosphere and the almost physical scent of heavy-foliaged tall trees, creating a vivid, fully Northern setting for the parting of Christ and his Mother, in whose swoon is fore-shadowed his death and her final grief. ›

13   JOHANN ROTTENHAMMER (1564-1625)
The Coronation of the Virgin   (6481)
Copper, 0.927 x 0.635 (36½ x 25)
Purchased 1983. Cleaned on acquisition

Born in Munich in 1564, Johann Rottenhammer travelled to Italy in 1589, spending the years until about 1595 in Rome. In Venice from about 1596, he transferred to Augsburg in 1606 where he became a sought-after and successful painter of large works. While in Italy he acted as host to German artists on their travels and thereby had contact with Adam Elsheimer whose hand may be detectable on this painting.

At the top of the painting the dove emits light on to a varied company of angels who surround and support a scene of the Virgin being crowned by God the Father and Christ. Saint John the Baptist kneels within this group, with his lamb at his feet. The Virgin lowers her eyes, her gaze meeting, one might think, that of Eve, who cranes her neck to look up. Sharing the same tier of heaven as she and her consort are, among others, Peter (with the keys, on the left), Paul, David, Moses and Jonah leaning on a fanciful whale.

Beneath them, on a lower tier, as propriety demands, are evangelists, saints and martyrs, including popes. Saint Luke is easily identifiable by his ox, as is Sebastian, whose arm is pierced by an arrow. The large figure, bottom right, is Saint Lawrence. Above him, dressed in a cope, is a bearded figure which has all the appearance of a portrait. Writing in 1963 (in the *Album Disciplorum J G van Gelder*), Ingrid Jost records Fritz Grossmann's identification of the figure as Camillo Borghese (1550-1605) who became a cardinal in 1596 and Pope Paul V in 1605.

A preparatory chalk drawing exists, measuring about two-thirds the size of the painting (Uffizi, Gabinetto dei Disegni, 0.602 x 0.414 (23¾ x 16¼). Squared up for transfer, its main compositional features are similar to those of the painting, but many differences exist, some noted by Jost. Most significant is the fact that Camillo Borghese does not appear.

Jost dates the drawing, by stylistic comparison, to the period encompassing the end of Rottenhammer's sojourn in Rome and the beginning of his time in Venice, namely 1595/96. Van Mander (*Het Leven der Doorluchtighe Nederlandsche en Hoogduytsche Schilders*, Haarlem 1604) describes "an All Saints picture, the first thing by which he gained a reputation...a large, upright painting on metal..." [The picture is certainly large for a copper panel.] Van Mander also implies that this painting was done in Rome, which would accord well with the presence of Borghese.

Against this hypothesis is, however, the inclusion of Saint Justina in the painting. A saint particularly revered in Venice and Padua, she does not bear her distinguishing attribute in the drawing. Finally, the character of the painting is wholly Venetian; it resembles nothing so much as a large Venetian altarpiece reduced to a miniature scale. Indeed, the division of the space into three vertical sections and the employment of Saints Jerome and Lawrence as largish coulisse figures is very like a *Coronation of the Virgin* (Venice, Accademia), attributed to Veronese or his workshop and executed about 1586 for the church of Ognissanti. The Venetian characteristics of the painting led Jost to postulate an earlier visit by Rottenhammer to Venice.

The painting was recorded at Althorp, home of the Spencer family, in 1822 (Dibden's *Aedes Althorpianae*) and probably earlier, and had probably come from the collection of the Earl of Arundel, advisor to King Charles I, in whose inventory of paintings, made in Amsterdam in 1655, it is probably mentioned. A marginal note made about 1671 by Hendrik Houmes in his copy of Van Mander refers to a *Coronation of the Virgin* by Rottenhammer as having been in the possession of Arundel when he was in Alkmaar.

The painting was acquired from the Spencer collection by Colnaghi & Co. from whom it was purchased by the National Gallery in 1983.

'The Gallery never sought desperately to represent Rottenhammer or sighed over the 'gap' his absence made. The chance to buy this outstanding and historically fascinating work by him was, however, quickly seized. It shows the impact of Venetian painting on a sensitive Northern temperament, and one would like to think that it is indeed the painting praised by van Mander and also the Rottenhammer that belonged to the Earl of Arundel, a great collector and connoisseur, 'one that loved and favored all artes and artists....'

14   CARAVAGGIO (1573-1610)
Boy Bitten by a Lizard   (6504)

Oil on canvas. 0.660 x 0.495 (26 x 19½)
Purchased, 1986. Cleaned on acquisition

When the young Caravaggio moved to Rome in the early 1590s he painted several pictures of loosely draped youths: these pictures were made expressly for selling, probably with a particular group of wealthy patrons in mind. The best known of these paintings are *Boy with a Basket of Fruit* (Rome, Galleria Borghese), *Bacchus* (Florence, Uffizi) and the National Gallery's *Boy Bitten by a Lizard*. This last, however, has an element of tension and drama not found in the other works in the group and is likely to have been made slightly later, at the end of the 1590s.

The subject was not entirely new — a popular 16th-century engraving shows a similar scene — but Caravaggio's treatment is highly original. The naturalism and startling effects of light caused a sensation in artistic circles in Rome. It was these early works that boosted Caravaggio's reputation, and led to his securing several major public commissions.

Another version of *Boy Bitten by a Lizard* exists in the Fondazione Longhi in Florence. Opinion had been divided as to which version was the original. But after the recent *Age of Caravaggio* exhibition at New York and Naples, scholars agreed that the painting purchased by the National Gallery is an autograph work of high quality.

A striking aspect of Caravaggio's art, especially in his early works, is still-life painting. In the National Gallery's *Supper at Emmaus* the still life is an important central element in the painting. In *Boy Bitten by a Lizard*, painted at around the same time, the still-life is particularly exquisite, showing a rose and some delicately handled jasmine in a glass vase in which the qualities of reflected light are meticulously observed.

The painting has been in Britain since at least the early 19th century, passing from the Methuen Collection to Viscount Harcourt's collection at Nuneham Park, where it was for a while attributed to Murillo (high praise at the time). Its acquisition for the nation is especially important at a time when both scholarly and popular interest in 17th-century Italian painting is increasing. It is the third painting by Caravaggio to enter the Collection and the last by the artist from a private collection in this country. The National Gallery's other paintings by Caravaggio, *The Supper at*

Emmaus and *Salome with the Head of John the Baptist*, are religious works very different in character to the *Boy Bitten by a Lizard*. Yet it was on such secular — or profane — works that Caravaggio's early reputation was based.

❛No stranger to controversy in his lifetime, Caravaggio would probably have enjoyed the art-historical controversies his work has given rise to since. Even before cleaning, the quality of this example was apparent. The still-life alone spoke of an autograph work, and as the painting was cleaned, Caravaggio's handling emerged the more unmistakeably. For comparison, one need only walk to look at the larger and later Supper at Emmaus, *a famous Caravaggio which came, as a gift, to the Collection surprisingly early in the 19th century.❜*

15 PETER PAUL RUBENS (1577-1640)
Samson and Delilah (6461)

Panel, 1.850 x 2.050 (72¾ x 80¾)
Purchased, 1980.

This magnificent painting belongs to the first years of Rubens' maturity. He was an artist who developed relatively slowly, using the eight years he spent in Italy (1600-1608) after his apprenticeship to develop and refine his art. Although a great reputation preceded the 31-year old painter back to Antwerp, he was in his first years in the city trying consciously to establish himself as a leading history painter. The *Samson and Delilah*, which was painted c. 1610/12, was probably commissioned from Rubens by Nicolaas Rockox, a wealthy merchant who had served nine times as burgomaster of Antwerp and whom Rubens described as 'my friend and patron' in a letter of May 1611. The evident care which Rubens took with this large painting was a direct result of the importance of the commission from Antwerp's leading Maecenas. The painting was in Rockox's possession by about 1613 when a print was made by Jacob Matham; a painting by Frans Francken the Younger of the 'great parlour' in Rockox's house shows the *Samson and Delilah* over the mantelpiece.

Italian memories are present throughout the painting. Rubens' study of the antique and of Michelangelo is clearly reflected in Samson's superbly muscled back and arm; Michelangelo's *Notte*, which Rubens had drawn, inspired the pose of Delilah, and the use of three distinct light sources recalls Caravaggio. Yet there is no doubt that the young painter had found his own quite individual artistic personality — the monumental composition, the profound characterisation of Delilah whose face and whose gesture with her left hand convey both triumph and pity, the rich application of paint (especially in the area of the central figures), the choice of a highly dramatic moment in the story, the unashamed eroticism — all these were to continue to be features of Rubens' art. There is a preparatory pen drawing for the painting in the van Regteren Altena collection in Amsterdam and an oil modello in the museum in Cincinnati.

The purchase of this major painting (perhaps the

major painting) of the years after Rubens' return from Italy added an important new dimension to the National Gallery's collection. Previously the great strengths of the Rubens collection had been the landscapes and the history paintings of the 1630s.

After leaving Rockox's collection the painting was acquired by the Prince of Liechtenstein from the Antwerp art dealers Forchoudt in 1700. It was sold by Prince Johann II in Paris in 1880. In 1929 the painting was rediscovered in Paris and published by Ludwig Burchard. It was sold in the following year to the Hamburg tobacco magnate, August Neuerburg. It was included in the Rubens exhibition at Antwerp, 1977 (No. 20). It was in the Neuerburg collection in Hamburg until its sale at Christie's on 11 July 1980. The purchase was made by Messrs Agnew acting on behalf of the National Gallery.

' *Although Rubens was collected in England and was represented in the Collection from its founding, his large-scale figure paintings remain rare over here, and the Gallery was weak in that area compared to the great Continental galleries. This masterpiece of Rubens's early maturity shows — one might say, shows off — all his abilities as majestic designer and colourist, brilliant, vigorous and also tender. Looking at these lovers, one is moved to murmur with the Chorus from Milton's* Samson Agonistes '*Yet beauty, though injurious, hath strange power.* '

---

16   ANTHONY VAN DYCK (1599-1641)
'The Balbi Children' (6502)

Canvas, 2.190 x 1.510 (86¼ x 59½)
Purchased, 1985.

Anthony van Dyck went to Italy late in 1621, when he was 22 years old. He travelled extensively in the peninsula and spent some months in Sicily but his base was always Genoa and in particular the house of his friends from Antwerp the brothers Cornelis and Lucas de Wael. Much of his travelling was done in his first three years in Italy and he then seems to have spent most of 1625-27 in Genoa, where he enjoyed great success as a portraitist to the local nobility. It is from this period that *'The Balbi Children'*, his most ambitious group portrait of children painted in Italy, dates.

The placing of the boys on steps between two imposing columns and beneath a looped-up curtain is a convention of Baroque portraiture; what distinguishes this painting is the individuality of the three boys, their vivacity of expression, their intimate compositional relationship and the virtuosity of the painting of their heads and their rich, embroidered clothes. Their pet choughs in the foreground add a further, lively element to the composition. As so often in Van Dyck's Genoese portraits, it is in the tension between the formality of the setting and the vivacity of the sitters that much of the painting's success resides.

The title of the painting is a traditional one and unfortunately we do not know exactly who the sitters are, although they are presumably brothers and members of one of the great aristocratic clans of Genoa. The portrait is mentioned for the first time in the 1740 inventory of the paintings inherited by Giacomo Balbi

from his father Costantino Balbi who had been Doge of Genoa from 1738 to 1740. (The Gallery's Luca Giordano of *Perseus turning Phineus and his followers to stone* and two of the Gallery's paintings by Rubens were also in this inventory.) *'The Balbi Children'* is presumably the "Ritratto di tre fanciulli del Vandik. palmi 10;

5,6" which has the very high valuation of 4000 lire (the Giordano was valued at 3000 and the *Chateau de Steen* at 2500). The use of the word "fanciulli" (rather than "mio zio .." or some other identification as appears elsewhere in the inventory) makes it unlikely that the sitters were related to Giacomo or Costantino Balbi. Costantino Balbi was an important collector and it is probably that he bought the painting from another aristocratic family in Genoa or from another of the many branches of his own family. It was purchased from a descendant of Giacomo Balbi, the Marchesa Violante Spinola, on behalf of William, 2nd Baron Berwick in 1824 or 1825. It hung at the Berwick family house, Attingham, until 1842 when it was sold through the dealer Woodburn to Thomas Philip, 2nd Earl de Grey. It was seen in Lord de Grey's London house by Gustav Waagen in 1851. Subsequently, the painting passed by marriage into the Cowper collection at Panshanger. It was exhibited at the Royal Academy in 1871 and at the Grosvenor Gallery in 1887. It came on loan to the National Gallery in 1909 and was here, with short breaks, until 1962. It was purchased from a descendent of Earl de Grey by private treaty sale in 1985 with the assistance of the J. Paul Getty II Endowment Fund.

‹ Through a reproduction, this painting had been familiar to me from childhood, and I inevitably find in it associations that add to its moving mixture of dignity and intimacy. Van Dyck's children are always effortlessly princely − perhaps because of some private self-identity of the artist's with race and breeding. I think only Velázquez equals Van Dyck's power to present the child as at once a proud dynastic pledge for the future and a fragile, immature, mortal creature. ›

---

17   FRANS HALS (c.1581-1666)
Young Man Holding a Skull   (6458)
Canvas, 0.922 x 0.808 (36¼ x 34½)
Purchased, 1980. Cleaned on acquisition

This outstanding example of Hals' bold, dramatic brushwork is, unusually in his work, not a portrait. It is intended as a vanitas, that is, a reminder of the certainty of death. It belongs to a Netherlandish tradition which goes back at least as far as Lucas van Leyden's engraving of 1516, also called *Young Man Holding a Skull*. It seems that this subject, more than conventional portraiture, gave Hals the opportunity to display his remarkable ability to conjure up form with a few slashing brushstrokes. The hand pointing out of the composition is especially daring. This painting should be dated about 1626/8. The boy's costume has nothing in common with the fashions of the day. The cloak thrown over his chest and the beret with its exaggeratedly long feather are clothes of a theatrical type which the Dutch followers of Caravaggio used in their allegorical and genre paintings.

The picture was included in the exhibition 'Art in Seventeenth-Century Holland', held at the National Gallery in 1976, and had been on loan to the Gallery until it was acquired. It complements the Gallery's important group of portraits by Frans Hals − six single portraits from all phases of his career and the large *Family Group in a Landscape* from the late 1640s.

The painting was purchased from the Trustees of the Elton Heirloom Settlement in 1980, with Christie's acting on behalf of the Settlement.

‹ The sheer bravura of this painting exercises its own appeal − and serves to lighten somewhat the effect of the more sober paintings by Hals previously representing him in the Collection. At the same time, its virtuosity should not be mistaken for flashiness, even if its solemn memento mori *message is largely counteracted by the liveliness of the paint and the artist's pleasure in his own accomplished performance. ›*

18 REMBRANDT VAN RIJN (1606-69)
Portrait of Hendrickje Stoffels (6432)

Signed (falsely), lower left: Rembrandt f./ 16(5 or 6) 9
Canvas, 1.019 x 0.835 (40¼ x 33¾)
Purchased 1976. Cleaned on acquisition

Hendrickje Stoffels was the artist's mistress. She entered the artist's household in 1649 as nurse to his young son, Titus. In 1654 she was summoned before the Council of the Reformed Church and admonished for living in sin with Rembrandt: the couple's only child, a daughter Cornelia, was born in the same year. Hendrickje remained in Rembrandt's household, through the financial crisis of the 1650s, until her death in 1663. There is no documented portrait of Hendrickje Stoffels but there are a number of paintings representing the same model and dating from the time when she was living with Rembrandt. The recurrence of this model and the affection and informality with which she is painted point to her being Hendrickje. *The Woman Bathing* of 1654, also in the National Gallery, is another of these paintings.

Stylistically, this painting belongs to a group of three-quarter length painted and etched portraits of the 1650s, in which Rembrandt can be seen experimenting with the pose and the spatial relationship between sitter, chair and picture space. It seems likely that it was at this time that Rembrandt informally painted Hendrickje in this pose. The X-rays reveal considerable changes in the pose and the position of the hands, which were at first both resting in her lap, probably clasped together. It may well be that a famous drawing by Rembrandt in the British Museum, showing a woman seated in a chair, leaning slightly forward, her hands clasped together, is preparatory to this painting. That drawing is usually dated about 1655/6 and this would be an acceptable date for the National Gallery painting: Hendrickje would have been aged between thirty and thirty-two. The signature and date on the painting were falsely added, perhaps in the early eighteenth century.

Certain formal aspects of the painting remain difficult to clarify: the precise nature of the material of Hendrickje's wrap, which is probably woollen; the table (or bed) sketched in the right foreground; and the background. Although these are all unfinished in the sense of a formal portrait, they did not perhaps need to be finished in an informal portrait of this kind.

The painting was purchased in Amsterdam in 1817 by the dealer William Buchanan. It entered the collection of James Morrison in 1835 and hung at his country seat, Basildon Park, Berkshire. It was purchased from the Trustees of the Walter Morrison Pictures Settlement by private treaty in January 1976, with the aid of a contribution from the National Art-Collections Fund.

The painting is more fully discussed by Christopher Brown and Joyce Plesters in *Apollo*, vol. 106, 1977, pp. 286-91.

'I find this portrait an unusually sympathetic Rembrandt, both as a piece of painting and for its subject. The sitter's pose has a touch of regality under apparent simplicity, much in the same way as her casual-seeming dress turns out to be accompanied by jewels glinting in her hair and ears. Even about the chair-arm there is a hint of sceptre. Hendrickje Stoffels is probably intended here to represent no-one but herself; about her hangs an air of pensiveness which Rembrandt records as if recognising it as part of her character.'

19 JAN STEEN (1625/6 - 79)
The Effects of Intemperance (6442)

Signed, lower left: JSteen (JS in monogram)
Panel, 0.760 x 1.065 (30 x 42)
Purchased, 1977. Cleaned on acquisition

The woman slumped on the left, whose purse is being picked by a child, is sleeping off the effects of alcohol. She illustrates the Dutch proverb *De Wijn is een spotter* (Wine is a mocker.) As in many other paintings by Steen, it is the foolishness of the elders which encourages the children to misbehave. Here the child throwing roses in front of the pig and the children feeding the cat illustrate popular sayings about foolish behaviour. In the background an old man is seducing a young girl, another of the pitfalls of alcohol. Above the head of the drunken women hangs a basket in which can be seen reminders of the fate of those who lack self-discipline − the crutch and clapper of the beggar and the birch of judicial punishment. Steen's moralistic message is that it is only by actively resisting the temptations of excessive indulgence in sensual pleasures that poverty and degredation can be avoided. And yet although the message is profoundly serious, the mood is one of amused disapproval rather than Puritanical revulsion.

Steen was an enormously prolific painter. Hectic activity in a career during which the artist was constantly on the move from town to town and frequently harrassed by creditors led not surprisingly to a marked unevenness in the quality of his output. At his best, as in this painting which was painted in about 1663/5, he is one of the greatest of all Dutch seventeenth-century painters.

When this painting was acquired in 1977 the Gallery already possessed no fewer than ten paintings by Steen, of which four − *A Young Woman Playing a Harpsichord, Music-Making on a Terrace, Grace before Meat*, and the magical *Skittleplayers outside an Inn* − are paintings of very high quality. All ten, however, are small paintings and give no idea of Steen's skill at composition on a large scale. This aspect of Steen's activity is now superbly represented by *The Effects of Intemperance*.

The painting was purchased from the Trustees of the Allendale Settlement by private treaty through Christie's, with the financial help of a group of anonymous benefactors.

'As a temperance tract this painting might succeed only in raising a laugh, but there is nothing funny or clumsy about the way Steen handles paint. Seeking less highly 'finished' effects than some of his contemporaries in Holland, he achieves greater subtlety and delicacy, especially in his treatment of materials like silk and satin, often anticipating Watteau in his response to textures.'

22

20 VELÁZQUEZ (1599-1660)
The Immaculate Conception (6424)

Canvas, 1.350 x 1.016 (53⅛ x 40)
Purchased, 1974.

The Virgin, crowned with twelve stars, stands upon a crescent moon; at her feet are symbols of her purity derived from the litanies of the Virgin, and here incorporated into the landscape.

The lower part of the drapery was at first designed differently as is visible from the painting, with a swirling fold of the cloak covering the lower part of the robe.

The picture is the same size and of the same date as *S. John the Evangelist on the Island of Patmos* (No. 6264). They are amongst the earliest of Velázquez's works, certainly painted before he moved from Seville to Madrid in 1623, and perhaps as early as 1618.

The two pictures are first recorded in 1800 as being in the Chapter House of the Convent of the Shod Carmelites at Seville. They were bought by Don Manuel Lopez Cepero, Dean of Seville, who sold them in 1809 to Bartholomew Frere, British Minister at Seville. The pictures were placed on loan at the National Gallery in 1946 by his descendants, Mrs Woodall and the Misses Frere; the *S. John* was acquired in 1956 and *The Immaculate Conception*, with the generous aid of the National Art Collections Fund and an anonymous donation, in 1974.

'*The acquisition of this painting followed a long period when it was generously lent to the Gallery, and for that reason, I presume, its purchase excited little press comment. No collection can have too many paintings by the artist (but thanks to government indifference, England lost a true heritage item in 1970, with the export of Velázquez' Juan de Pareja). The* Immaculate Conception *is an early work, of course, but already it is invested with the sober gravity and weight, in both pictorial and metaphorical senses, that mark every painting Velázquez touched and which defy description.* '

21   BARTOLOME ESTEBAN MURILLO
(1617-82)

Portrait of Don Justino de Neve   (6448)

Inscribed below the sitter's coat of arms: ETATIS
SVAE.40 / Bartholome Murillo Romulensis / Praecirca
obsequium desiderio pingebat / A. M. [D.] C. L. X. V.
Canvas, 2.060 x 1.295 (81⅛ x 51)
Purchased, 1979. Cleaned shortly before acquisition

The sitter was a canon and prebendary of the Cathedral
of Seville, and a close friend of the artist. He was
instrumental in commissioning the series of canvases
by Murillo in S. Maria la Blanca (1662-65) and those in
the Hospital of the Venerables (1678), and he also
acted as one of the three executors of Murillo's will.

The coat of arms (of the Neve and Chaves family)
and the inscription, which became fully visible after
cleaning, are probably early additions to the picture.
The date, 1665, is in accordance with the style of the
painting, though before cleaning it was usually dated to
the late 1670s. The third line of the inscription
apparently refers to work being carried out by Murillo
for Don Justino at this time, presumably in S. Maria la
Blanca: 'Murillo / was painting [this] at the request [of
the sitter while] in [his] service.' 'Romulensis' would
refer to the Roman name for Seville, 'Colonia
Romulensis'.

No. 6448, which is Murillo's only known seated
full-length, has always been regarded as the masterpiece among his portraits, and it represents one of the
few aspects of his art not already shown to advantage in
the collection. Early writers singled out in particular
the dog at Don Justino's feet, an English lap-dog 'una
perilla inglese' (a pug?), the still-life (the clock registers
ten to four), and the appearance of the sitter himself. A
fuller account of the portrait by Allan Braham appears
in *The Burlington Magazine*, March, 1980, pp.192-94,
and in *Agnew: A Dealer's Record*, 1981, pp.98-102.

The portrait was left to the Hospital of the Vener-
ables in Don Justino's will (1685) and it is recorded in
the 18th century as hanging in the ante-refectory there.
One of the many Sevillian paintings confiscated in 1810
on behalf of King Joseph Bonaparte, it was imported to
England before 1818 and acquired by the collector and
Member of Parliament, George Watson Taylor. Bought
at his sale at Erlestoke Park in 1832 by the Marquess of
Lansdowne and thence by descent. Acquired through
Sir Geoffrey Agnew of Agnew's from the Trustees of the
Bowood Collection, 1979.

❛*This unique full-length portrait comes as a surprise
to anyone who thinks of the painter as a purveyor of
sentimental, weakly pretty religious paintings. It is
grander than his restrained* Self-Portrait *in the Collection and returns one to the world of Titian. Fine in
itself, it may also serve to send people to look again at
the range of Murillo's work in the Gallery and to
rediscover, or just discover, an under-estimated
artist.* ❜

22 CLAUDE GELLEE (1600-82)
*'The Enchanted Castle' (Psyche outside
the Palace of Cupid)* (6471)

Canvas, 0.870 x 1.510 (34½ x 59½)
Purchased, 1981.

The Gallery is rich in the work of Claude, but *'The
Enchanted Castle'* is of a rare, late type that epitomises
the artist's qualities as a painter of mood and atmos-
phere. While not his largest or grandest work, it is
probably his most celebrated. The title 'The Enchanted
Castle' dates from Woollett's engraving of 1782 and
aptly reflects the mysterious mood of the picture which
made it so popular in England with the artists, writers
and poets of the Romantic movement.

Claude painted the picture in 1664 for Lorenzo
Onofrio Colonna, Constable of Naples, and the composition is recorded in the Liber Veritatis (no. 162).
Baldinucci refers to it as 'Psyche on the Seashore', and in
1665 Claude painted a pendant for Colonna of *Psyche
saved from drowning herself*, (L.V. 167), now in the
Wallraf-Richartz Museum, Cologne. The subjects are
derived from Apuleius' account of the story of Cupid
and Psyche in *The Golden Ass*; the earlier picture is
probably intended to show Psyche after she has disco-
vered Cupid's identity, when he has abandoned her.

The two paintings came to England some time
between 1720 and 1777, when they are recorded as
belonging to Dr N. Chauncey. For a brief period they
belonged to Charles Alexandre Calonne, emigré Prime
Minister of France, until in 1795 they were sold with
the rest of his collection, going to different buyers. *'The
Enchanted Castle'* subsequently passed through various hands before entering the Loyd collection in
about 1850, when it was bought by Lord Overstone.

'The Enchanted Castle' has always been especially
highly regarded. Baldinucci wrote of its 'outstanding
beauty', and later commentators such as Hazlitt, Ruskin
and Waagen, all remark on its poetic quality. John Keats
writes of it at length in a verse letter of 25 March 1818 to
his friend J.H. Reynolds, representing the castle as a
sinister and melancholy place of magical enchantment.
The picture also left its mark on one of Keats' great odes,
the Ode to a Nightingale of 1819. The 'magic case-
ments, opening on the foam/Of perilous seas, in faery
lands forlorn' seem to be prompted by the image of the
castle with its open window and the sea beyond. The
picture was on exhibition at the British Institution
when Keats wrote his ode, and as an admirer of Claude
and a friend of painters, he would almost certainly have
seen it there.

The painting was the subject of the first Acquisition in Focus exhibition, by Michael Wilson (1982), and it was subsequently included in the Claude Lorrain exhibition in Washington and Paris (1982-83, No. 45). It was offered by the Loyd Trustees through Thomas Agnew and Sons Ltd., having been on loan since 1974; it was purchased by private treaty in June 1981 with the help of generous grants from the National Heritage Memorial Fund and the NACF.

'Keats and Hazlitt are among those who have testified to the overwhelming spell cast by this painting, and here silence seems the best tribute. If 'heritage' has any significance or relevance where non-British works of art are concerned, this is a supreme 'heritage' item, outstanding for its literary associations — and also for its beauty.'

23 JEAN-BAPTISTE PERRONNEAU
(1715(?)-83)
Portrait of Jacques Cazotte (6435)

Signed, upper right: Perroneau
Canvas, 0.921 x 0.730 (36¼ x 28¾)
Purchased, 1976. Cleaned on acquisition

The sitter was a writer of verse, romantic novels and fantastic oriental tales. He was born in Dijon in 1719 and in September 1747 obtained a public appointment in Martinique. He was in France between July 1752 and January 1754 and returned again finally in 1759, settl-

ing after 1760 on an estate in the village of Pierry, near Epernay, in Champagne. It is possible that Perronneau, whose family had property in the same area, met and painted him there. In August 1792, after the discovery of compromising letters against the Revolution, Cazotte was arrested. He was guillotined on 25 September.

The present portrait shows Perroneau's outstanding grasp of physiognomy and reveals him as no less a master than his more famous contemporary, La Tour. Unlike La Tour, however, Perronneau did not work in pastel alone, frequently painting in oils. A replica or copy of the portrait of Cazotte is in the municipal collection at Chalons-sur-Marne. Perronneau's work is rare in this country, and the National Gallery may be the only English public collection to possess examples by him. The portrait of Cazotte, formerly in the collection of Mrs Meyer Sassoon, was purchased at Christie's on 2 July 1976.

'The Gallery's reluctance for many years to purchase French 18th-century paintings is most charitably explained by over-consciousness of the Wallace Collection, where, as it happens, male portraiture is not a strength. Perronneau can be more brusquely direct than his famous contemporary La Tour and his equal in capturing the fleeting, quizzical expression on a face. He conjures up Cazotte with wonderful vivacity, and seems to convey a sense of the period Cazotte typifies as well as the individual.'

24 FRANCOIS-HUBERT DROUAIS (1727-75)
Madame de Pompadour (6440)

Signed on work-table to right: Peint par Drouais le fils/la
tete en avril 1763: et le/tableau fini en mai 1764
Canvas, 2.170 x 1.568 (85⅞ x 61⅝)
Purchased, 1977.

The sitter, Jeanne-Antoinette Poisson was born in
1721, and in 1741 married Charles-Guillaume Le Nor-
mant d'Etoiles. In 1745 she became the mistress of
Louis XV, and was created Marquise de Pompadour. She
exercised considerable influence on the public policy
of France and was a great patron of the arts and letters.
Among those she supported and patronised were
Voltaire and Boucher.

This large full-length portrait was begun in 1763
when she was 41, and not completed until some weeks
after her death on 5 April 1764. The head appears to
have been painted on a separate rectangle that was then
joined to the rest of the canvas. The Marquise appears in
a lace cap and a lavishly embroidered silk dress edged
with lace, and is seated on a canapé. Around her are
signs of her varied pursuits: a mandolin, an artist's folio
and a bookcase. To her left is an elaborate work-table
and she is shown embroidering on a frame, observed by
her pet dog.

The painting is the first female portrait of the
French eighteenth century of this scale and importance
to enter the National Gallery. Smaller portraits of
Madame de Pompadour by Boucher can be seen in the
Victoria & Albert Museum and the Wallace Collection.
In its unaffectedness and in the emphasis it places upon
the Marquise's accomplishments and industry, the
picture is characteristic of French portraiture after the
middle of the century.

A contemporary, Bachaumont, saw the picture at
the artist's studio in August 1764 and noted 'We have
seen for some weeks at the Palais des Tuileries the large
portrait of the late Marquise de Pompadour by Drouais,
painter of reputation. The resemblance is one of the
most striking and the composition of the painting is as
rich as you would expect'.

The picture entered England some time after
1845. Baron Meyer de Rothschild purchased it in 1869
at the John Webb sale and it passed through the
marriage of his daughter into the Rosebery family. It
was purchased at the time of the Mentmore House sale
by the Gallery from the Earl of Rosebery by private
treaty in 1977.

*❛In 1977 Treasury ministers rejected advice to accept
this painting for the nation, in lieu of tax. It is a tribute
to the then owner and his advisers that they retained
sufficient patience to agree a private treaty sale with
the Gallery instead of sending the painting to auction.
The portrait is a triumph of artistic skill, quite apart
from its interest as the last portrait from life of
Madame de Pompadour. No wanton favourite of a
king here, she has become the incarnation of
bourgeois virtue and industry. Alone, apart from a pet
dog, rouged perhaps to conceal illness and bravely
dressed-up as though cheering herself up, she seems
determinedly occupied and unaware of how short her
existence was to be. ❜*

25 JEAN-HONORE FRAGONARD
(1732-1806)
Psyche showing her sisters her gifts from Cupid (6445)
Canvas, 168.3 x 192.4 (66¼ x 75¾)
Purchased, 1978. Cleaned shortly before acquisition

Except for one small genre scene ascribed to Fragonard (No. 2620), this is the first painting by the artist to have entered the Collection. There are few of his works in Britain in public or private hands, and no large mythological compositions of this type. Although cut down slightly on the top and left sides, the condition is good. A pentimento of a large urn, is visible in the centre.

No. 6445 depicts an episode from the classical myth of Cupid and Psyche, probably best known to Fragonard through La Fontaine's *Les Amours de Psyché et de Cupidon*. Psyche is portrayed with attendants and putti, showing the rich gifts that she has received from Cupid to her two sisters. They jealously try to wreck her happiness by destroying her faith in her invisible lover. One of the Furies is depicted, serpent-haired, hovering above the sisters, inspiring them with envy.

The picture was painted in 1753, shortly after the young Fragonard had left the studio of Boucher to enter the Ecole Royale des Elèves Protégés, to which he was admitted after winning the Grand Prix de Rome in 1752

with *Jereboam sacrificing to the Idols* (The Louvre). There is a strong resemblance in composition and handling between the two pictures. However, the *Psyche*, being better suited in subject to Fragonard's temperament, is both more accomplished and more indicative of his later development.

The painting was exhibited at Versailles in January 1754 with works by Fragonard's fellow pupils, and there seen by Louis XV. Its later history is not fully established and it was assumed lost until, in 1977, it appeared in the Earl of Rosebery sale at Mentmore, catalogued as *The Toilet of Venus* by Carle Van Loo, Fragonard's master at the Ecole Royale. It was purchased by the dealer, Mr David Carritt, who suspected it to be by Fragonard, and, after cleaning, identified by him as the lost picture. It was sold to the Gallery by a subsidiary of Artemis S A in April 1978 and acquired with the help of a group of anonymous benefactors.

'*It is tempting to re-title this painting 'Fragonard showing his brother-pupils his artistic gifts', for its youthful ability and exuberance are so patent. Even if it is not entirely successful, and inevitably not entirely original, it announces the arrival of a new talent on the artistic scene in France, bringing welcome energy at a period of artistic uncertainty and some lassitude.* '

26   JACQUES-LOUIS DAVID (1748-1825)
Jacobus Blauw   (6495)

Canvas, 0.920 x 0.730 (36¼ x 28¾)
Signed, bottom left: L. DAVID. 4
Inscribed, on the sheet of paper: J. BLAUW, ministre
Plénipotentiaire aux Etats Généraux des provinces
unies
Purchased, 1984.

This is the first painting by David to enter the Collection, and the first work by the artist in any British public collection. David trained under Vien and won the Prix de Rome in 1774. He was in Rome from 1775 to 1780 and on his return to Paris achieved the reputation of leader of the Neoclassical school with the success of his *Belisarius* (1781), *The Oath of the Horatii* (1785), *The Death of Socrates* (1787) and the *Brutus* (1789). He actively participated in the Revolution, was elected a Deputy and was responsible for the abolition of the Académie. In 1794/5, following the fall of Robespierre, he was imprisoned. He later became premier peintre to Napoleon, and after the fall of Napoleon, went into exile in Brussels where he died.

The sitter, Jacobus Blauw (1756-1829), was a leading Dutch Patriot who in 1795 helped to establish the Batavian Republic. When the French army invaded the Netherlands, Blauw was sent to Paris to negotiate a peace settlement, but only after the Treaty of The Hague was signed on 16 May 1795 was he officially recognised as ministre plénipotentiaire. It was probably then that he and his fellow Dutch minister, Caspar Meyer, commissioned David to paint their portraits (the portrait of Meyer is in the Louvre). David, however, was imprisoned for a second time from 29 May until 3 August and probably did not execute Blauw's portrait until October or November. The portrait is dated 4 (year four of the French Republic), and a letter from Blauw thanking David for the portrait and expressing his devotion and esteem for the artist is dated 8 Frimaire An IV (29 November, 1975).

Blauw later served as ministre plénipotentiaire in Venice, Genoa and Turin, and again in 1798 as a Dutch representative in Paris. Although with the coup of 12 June 1798 he was dismissed from his post, he continued to live for the most part in Paris, where he died in 1829. Further details about the sitter and the portrait are given by Michael Wilson in *The Burlington Magazine*, 1984, pp.694-98.

The portrait of Blauw remained in the possession of his descendants in France until sold to a firm of Paris dealers, after having been on loan to the Musée des Beaux-Arts de Dijon. After prolonged negotiations with the French authorities, who in recognition of the especial importance of the painting to Britain eventually agreed to its export, it was purchased by the Gallery in 1984.

❛ *Artist and sitter seem locked in deep* rapport *in this typically disciplined, precisely crafted and beautifully preserved portrait. It is not merely the face of Jacobus Blauw that David seizes and fixes but the line of his linen, the stiffness of his quill-pen and the very sit of his coat, with its coin-like, metallic buttons, each burnished in paint. No area is without its vibrant touch, but perhaps most masterly of all is the background, neutral-seeming yet not dull, almost palpitating and with its own vitality to match that of the sitter.* ❜

27 LUIS MELÉNDEZ (1716-80)
Still Life with Oranges and Walnuts (6505)

Signed and dated 1772
Oil on canvas, 0.610 x 0.813 (24 x 32)
Purchased, 1985.

The painting is one of a group of the artist's largest and finest works: two others are in the Boston Museum of Fine Arts and another in a private collection in the United States. It is the first painting by Meléndez to enter the National Gallery.

Meléndez was the foremost painter of still-lifes in Spain during the 18th century. Along with Luis Paret and Francisco Bayeu he was one of the most accomplished Spanish painters of his generation apart from Goya.

Born in Naples the young Luis moved with his family back to Madrid where his father, also a painter, was one of the instigators of the new Academy of San Fernando. Unfortunately, the elder Meléndez quarelled bitterly and publicly with the other Academicians which resulted in the expulsion of both father and son. Until then Luis had been working as a portrait painter; to judge from the self-portrait of 1746 now in the Louvre he was extremely talented in this genre.

When Luis Meléndez turned to still-life painting is not known: his earliest signed and dated still life is from 1759. During the 1760s he painted the forty five pictures that hung in the Royal Palace at Aranjuez: this series represents half Meléndez's known oeuvre, and is mainly now at the Museo del Prado in Madrid.

The Aranjuez series provides a convenient yard-stick for judging Meléndez's work. The paintings are small but the objects depicted appear solid and monumental within a compact but relaxed composition. In many of his larger paintings this quality of compactness is often lost, the composition becomes more rambling. In the gallery's *Still-life with Oranges and Walnuts* Meléndez has managed to combine scale with the particular quality of his smaller work.

The subtle earth colours of the nuts, boxes and pottery are cleverly balanced with the bright oranges and dry green melon in the background. The clear, frank treatment of everyday objects recalls Spanish still-life painting of the 17th century. Although comparison with his French near contemporary, Chardin, is perhaps inevitable, Meléndez's approach is uniquely Spanish: while the objects are composed and depicted with such apparent sobriety, there is an element of mystery in the painting. This is probably unintended. But it is a feature of much great Spanish painting and it is likely that Meléndez, like Goya, was keenly aware of the traditions of painting in Spain.

❛ We deliberately took some years considering before finally selecting our Meléndez – with almost as much care, perhaps, as the painter took in selecting the objects for one of his still-lives. What we wanted was an example that in scale and artistic concentration (as well as in condition) would be worthy of the National Gallery Collection. That set a very high standard, which this painting simply, uncontestably, meets. ❜

28   LUIS PARET (1746-1799)
View of El Arenal de Bilbao   (6489)
Panel 0.603 x 0.832 (23¾ x 32¾)
Signed and dated, 1784, three times (lower left)
Purchased, 1983.

It is almost certain that the *View of El Arenal de Bilbao* is one of a series of paintings depicting the Cantabrian ports of Spain. The series was commissioned from Paret in 1786 by King Charles III but was in fact begun several years earlier (about 1781) on the instructions of the King's son, the Prince of Asturias (who became Charles IV in 1789). The commission received official status only after the death in 1785 of Paret's former disgraced royal patron, Don Luis de Borbón.

The model for this series was a similar commission in 1753, again royal, to Joseph Vernet in France for a series of views of French ports, paintings which the Prince of Asturias knew and wished to have emulated in his own country. The clear French element in Paret's style shows the domination by French artists of painting in the Iberian peninsula since the Borbón accession in 1713. One of Paret's several teachers was French and it is possible (but not documented) that he visited Paris while returning to Madrid from Rome in 1766.

Paret's highly successful early career, working in Court circles, was interrupted by his involvement in a scandal concerning his patron, Don Luis de Borbón, brother of King Charles III. This led in 1775 to three years of exile in Puerto Rico after which he was permitted to return to Spain but not Madrid. He settled in Bilbao and two years later, in 1780, was elected to the Academia de San Fernando in Madrid (although still not permitted to return to the city).

The *Puertos de Cantabria* are recorded by Ceán Bermúdez as being divided between the Royal Palace in Madrid and the Casino del Rey at the Escorial. There were at least six. The series was dispersed in 1808 during the Napoleonic war. No. 6489, one of the most sensitive and accomplished of Paret's known landscape paintings, shows what now forms the centre of modern Bilbao, on the river Nervion. In the distance, towards the left, is the convent of Saint Agustin, since demolished to make way for the present city hall.

No. 6489 passed through Christie's on 24 March 1922 (lot 111). It subsequently entered the collection of the Hon. Bertram Bell near Dublin and was auctioned again at Christie's on 2 December 1983 (lot 77). It was purchased by Mr Jack Baer of Hazlitt, Gooden and Fox Ltd., acting on behalf of the National Gallery. Another painting by Paret from the *Puertos de Cantabria* series was also sold at Christie's on 2 December 1983 (lot 76). It is a *View of Bermeo*, signed and dated 1783, and at the time of publication is on long term loan to the Gallery.

'*It is nice to introduce a 'new' painter to the Collection and also to awareness of our public. Apart from Goya, 18th century Spanish painting is little known or seen outside Spain. Paret is only one among a number of interesting painters of the period, though one of the most sprightly − almost Guardi-like at times, enlivening his views, as here, with vivid, silvery little figures.*'

29   GEORGE STUBBS (1724-1806)
The Milbanke and Melbourne Families   (6429)

Canvas, 0.972 x 1.493 (38¼ x 58¾)
Purchased, 1975.

The sitters are traditionally identified. They were related by marriage and are from left to right: Elizabeth Milbanke, later first Viscountess Melbourne, her father Sir Ralph Milbanke, Bt., her brother, John Milbanke, and Sir Peniston Lamb, first Viscount Melbourne. Elizabeth Milbanke married Sir Peniston Lamb in April 1769 and the picture was probably painted soon afterwards to commemorate the marriage. It seems likely that *The Milbanke and Melbourne Families* is the painting exhibited as *A Conversation* at the Society of Artists' exhibition in 1770.

Elizabeth Milbanke was only seventeen when she married and the couple's first son Peniston was born in May 1770; their second son, William, was the famous Lord Melbourne who became prime minister. Sir Ralph Milbanke was the grandfather through his eldest son of Anne Isabella Milbanke who married Byron.

For a detailed description of the sitters see the entry for this painting in the Tate Gallery exhibition catalogue, *George Stubbs 1724-1806* (1984).

The picture seems first recorded at Panshanger, home of the Cowper family, in the nineteenth century. The 5th Earl married Emily Lamb, daughter of the first Viscount and Viscountess Melbourne. The picture descended in the family until its sale in 1975 to Marlborough Fine Art Ltd. An export licence for it was refused by the Reviewing Committee and the picture purchased by the Gallery in 1975.

❛ Today Stubbs is appreciated at his true value but it has taken a long time for depreciating and patronising attitudes to vanish. No effort was made in the 19th century to put his work in the National Gallery, and he was represented by just one painting (given in 1920) before acquisition of the Milbanke and Melbourne *families. If a single painting can crystallise all Stubbs' qualities, this one has good claim to do so. ❜*

30 JOSEPH WRIGHT OF DERBY (1734-97)
Mr and Mrs Thomas Coltman   (6496)

Oil on canvas, 1.270 x 1.016 (50 x 40)
Purchased, 1984. Cleaned on acquisition

Joseph Wright is best known for his candle-light pictures, and for his depiction of contemporary scenes of scientific and industrial interest, such as *The Experiment with an Air Pump* (No. 725). However, he also painted landscapes and subject pictures, and the greater part of his work consists of portraits. He was born at Derby, and trained in London under Thomas Hudson. On returning to Derby, he established himself as a portrait painter. He visited Italy from 1773 to 1775 and on his return spent two years in Bath before taking up residence again in Derby, where he remained until his death.

The portrait was painted for Thomas Coltman (1746-1826), a Lincolnshire landowner who is shown with his first wife, Mary Barlow, whom he had married in 1769 and who died in 1788. It must have been painted soon after the marriage, probably in the spring of 1771 or 1772, before Wright's Italian journey. Thomas Coltman was a close friend of Wright and he eventually owned four paintings by the artist.

In his monograph *Joseph Wright of Derby* (1968), Benedict Nicolson describes the painting as an 'undoubted masterpiece'. He stresses the uniting in it of portraiture, animal painting and landscape: 'here for the first time [in Wright's work] landscape comes into its own'. He also relates the painting to Stubbs' *Milbanke and Melbourne Families*, purchased by the Gallery in 1975, which may have suggested Coltman's pose, leaning against his wife's horse. Wright, however, had a life-long passion for classical art and the pose of Coltman recalls the statues of the Quirinal Horse-Tamers in Rome and the Borghese Gladiator. A model of the latter sculpture was the subject of *The Gladiator*, the first of Wright's famous night scenes. The pose of Mary Barlow may also derive from a statue in the Borghese collection, known as the *The Nymph with a Shell*, a sculpture which Wright had earlier depicted in *An Academy by Lamplight*.

The painting is in excellent condition on an unlined canvas and the cleaning revealed the quality of the artist's technique. Wright's skill at rendering light effects is evident in the sky and landscape, and in the very naturalistic sunlight illuminating the foreground group.

In Wright's account book for 1770/71 it is recorded that the painting was sold to Mr and Mrs Coltman for £63. It remained in the sitters' family until it was sent for auction at Christie's on 23rd November 1984. It was purchased by Agnew's, acting for the Gallery, with the aid of grants from the National Heritage Memorial Fund and the Pilgrim Trust. In 1986 the painting was the subject of a National Gallery Acquisition in Focus exhibition, organised by Allan Braham, who also wrote an accompanying booklet.

'The label 'of Derby' hangs heavily around Wright's reputation, encouraging suggestions perhaps of the provincial or the minor (if the two are not anyway equated). This unprovincial double portrait is a masterpiece in a thoroughly British vein, deserving of its place alongside comparable paintings by Gainsborough and Stubbs, and also within a European context. '

31 FERDINAND-VICTOR-EUGENE DELACROIX (1798-1863)
Christ on the Cross   (6433)

Signed and dated at base of Cross: Eug. Delacroix 1853
Canvas, 0.735 x 0.597 (28⅞ x 23½)
Purchased, 1976.

Before the purchase of this picture, the Gallery possessed only two major works by Delacroix, the leading exponent of romantic painting in France: the early portrait of Baron Schwiter, and the late *Ovid among the Scythians*. As a painting of considerable emotional and dramatic quality, and as a religious work, the present picture is highly representative of the production of Delacroix's mature years.

Delacroix had exhibited a larger picture of this subject at the Salon of 1835 (now at the Vannes Museum) showing Christ between the two thieves, and another smaller version, closer in design to the present picture, at the Salon of 1847 (now in the Walters Art Gallery, Baltimore). However, each picture can be considered an independent composition, and of the three it is the National Gallery picture which seems to represent Delacroix's final thoughts on the subject. It is reduced to absolute essentials, with barely a suggestion of landscape, although the presence of Judas in the right foreground is highly unusual.

The composition may well have been inspired by Pierre-Paul Prud'hon's painting of the same subject, which is dated 1822, and is now in the Louvre. In his journal for 1853 Delacroix recalls his pleasure at having seen a copy of the Prud'hon some years previously.

The picture is said to have been bought from the painter for 1,200 francs by a Monsieur Beugniet on 18 July 1853. Since then it has been in various French private collections until purchased by the Gallery from the Paris firm of Daber, 1976.

The painting is No. 1223 in *l'Oeuvre Complet de Eugène Delacroix* by A. Robaut (1885).

'The murals of Saint-Sulpice show what a great religious painter Delacroix was. That is something of a rarity in the 19th century. He could make art out of the always difficult subject of the Crucifixion, and small though the present painting is, it has an almost cosmic air of grief and desolation. Each time Delacroix tackled the theme, he re-thought it. His brain seethed with ideas, as he himself put it, writing sadly in the last, illness-ridden months of his life.'

32   HILAIRE-GERMAIN-EDGAR DEGAS
(1834-1917)
Hélène Rouart in her father's study   (6469)

Stamp of the Degas sale, bottom right
Canvas, 1.610 x 1.200 (63⅜ x 47¼)
Purchased, 1981.

Hélène Rouart was the only daughter of Degas' lifelong friend Henri Rouart (1833-1912) who himself painted and exhibited at seven of the eight Impressionist group shows. Degas had painted her as a girl on her father's knee in about 1877 (Heinemann collection, New York) and the present portrait was completed in 1886, when Hélène was apparently eighteen. According to her brother, Louis, the picture was the outcome of a project to paint the whole Rouart family. Jean Boggs suggests that Degas planned in 1884 to paint Hélène with her mother, and two pastels and a drawing survive showing Hélène standing, wrapped in a shawl, admiring a Tanagra figurine with her mother. Perhaps due to Madame Rouart's ill health, Degas later decided to paint Hélène alone in her father's study or library in the family house on the rue de Lisbonne. A number of preparatory drawings show her seated on the arm of the chair that appears in the final picture.

The portrait of Hélène Rouart is one of several by Degas showing a sitter in an interior which extends and reflects his or her personality. In this instance the objects surrounding Hélène belong to her father who was a notable collector. On the left, in a glass case, are Egyptian wood statues, the nearest being a Ptah-Seker-Osiris or funerary deity of the late New Kingdom. High on the wall is a Chinese silk hanging probably of the 19th century, and on the right are two pictures, an oil study of *The Bay of Naples and the Castello dell'Ovo* by Corot, painted in 1828, and below it a drawing by Millet of a seated peasant woman.

Degas presents Hélène as someone nurtured in a cultivated environment, and he evokes the father's presence not only in the objects from his collection but also in the large empty chair upon which Hélène rests her hands.

The picture is broad in execution and reveals a number of *pentimenti*, particularly in the contours of the figure and in the costume. However, it is not necessarily unfinished. It does not seem to have been a commission, and considering his strong links with the Rouart family, Degas could well have painted it for himself.

It remained in Degas' studio until his death and was purchased in 1918 by Rosenberg at the first Degas sale, where it was wrongly titled *La Visite au Musée*. In 1924 it was purchased by René Gimpel whose son, Mr Peter Gimpel, agreed to sell the picture to the Gallery by private treaty in April 1981.

The picture is discussed in detail in J.S. Boggs *Portraits by Degas* (1962) and T. Reff, *Degas: The Artist's Mind* (1976). It has appeared in various exhibitions including the 1979/80 Post-Impressionism exhibition at the Royal Academy, and at the National Gallery of Art, Washington. In 1984 the painting was the subject of a National Gallery *Acquisition in Focus* exhibition organised by Dillian Gordon, who also wrote an accompanying booklet.

'More than one Degas enthusiast had privately urged us in recent years to acquire this painting, if we could. While I needed no urging with regard to the painter, I may confess that I was unsure how well the painting would look hung in the Gallery, hankering, it may be, for one of Degas's earlier, less 'difficult' portraits. When the opportunity unexpectedly came, the painting proved to take its place in a magisterial way, impressive not only in scale but in its very complexity.'

33 CAMILLE PISSARRO (1830-1903)
The Avenue, Sydenham (6493)

Signed and dated, bottom left: C. Pissarro 1871
Canvas, 0.480 x 0.730 (19 x 28¾)
Purchased, 1984.

This painting is one of twelve which Pissarro is known to have painted during his residence in London in 1870/71. Another, *Lower Norwood under Snow*, is also in the Collection (No. 3265). There is a watercolour study for No. 6493 in the Louvre. To escape the effects of the Franco-Prussian war, Pissarro fled with his family, first to Brittany, and then to London, where he settled in Upper Norwood, close to relatives. In London he made contact with Monet and with Paul Durand-Ruel, who bought four of his pictures and included them in his London exhibitions. His work was rejected by the Royal Academy but included in the French section of the 1871 International Exhibition at South Kensington.

The present picture is the largest (by a small margin) of the London paintings and represents The Avenue, a broad, tree-lined street in the suburb of Sydenham, near the re-located Crystal Palace (the subject of a painting in the Art Institute, Chicago) and Upper Norwood, where Pissarro was living. The church of Saint Bartholomew on Westwood Hill, visi-

ble in the distance, still remains, but the character of Lawrie Park Avenue (as it was renamed in 1886) is much altered, with modern housing replacing the former large villas. In Pissarro's painting the trees are shown just coming into leaf, suggesting it was painted in about April 1871.

The Avenue, Sydenham was purchased by Paul Durand-Ruel, almost certainly in London in 1871, and remained with the Galerie Durand-Ruel until some time between 1924 and 1932. It entered a private collection in Switzerland before May 1938, from which it was sold by auction at Christie's on 26 March 1984, where it was purchased by Lefevre's for the Gallery.

The picture is catalogued in L.R. Pissarro and L. Venturi, *Camille Pissarro, son art et son oeuvre* (1939).

'Destruction everywhere' was one report on the state of Paris at about the time Pissarro painted this peaceful impression of a spring day in a London suburb. The sense of contrast is so strong that I feel he must have been expressing, consciously or not, his feelings of relief at finding himself safely away from the horrors of France in the aftermath of the Franco-Prussian war. Everything in the painting is vernal and succulent, and reassuring. Yet it is no casual sketch but skilfully composed and plotted, artful in its very air of spontaneity.

34   CLAUDE MONET (1840-1926)
The Gare St. Lazare   (6479)

Signed bottom right: Claude Monet
Canvas, 0.540 x 0.730 (21¼ x 28¾)
Purchased, 1982.

This painting is one of a group of the Gare St-Lazare and the tracks just outside the station which Monet painted in the early part of 1871. According to Jean Renoir, Monet obtained permission from the Director of the Chemins de fer de l'Ouest to paint inside the Gare St-Lazare. He began work in January 1877 and in April he exhibited seven paintings of the station and its environs (including possibly the present example) at the Third Impressionist Exhibition. There they received special praise from Emile Zola and Georges Rivière.

Four of the group are painted from within the station: two (in the Jeu de Paume and the Fogg Art Museum) show the suburban lines, the other two (the present painting and another of similar composition in the Art Institute of Chicago) show the main lines, in the eastern part of the station, bordering on the rue d'Amsterdam. They are remarkable not only as depictions of the contemporary urban scene but also as characteristically Impressionist description of atmos-phere, with the forms of buildings, locomotives and people obscured and transformed in the steam, smoke and light.

This view of the Gare St-Lazare was first owned by Lazare Weiller. At the sale of his collection in 1901 it was bought by Oscar Schmitz of Dresden, and in 1936 it was sold by Wildenstein to Samuel Courtauld. It was purchased by the Gallery, by private treaty, in 1982.

The painting is included in D. Wildenstein, *Claude Monet, Biographie et Catalogue Raisonné*, vol. 1 (1974). For an analysis of the palette used by Monet in *The Gare St-Lazare*, see Ashok Roy, 'The Palettes of Three Impressionist Paintings' in the *National Gallery Technical Bulletin*, vol. 9, 1985.

❛ *The railway is a phenomenon entirely created by the 19th century, and it is impossible not to think of its appearance in literature of the period as well as in painting. Monet's concern with it, however, could hardly be less dramatic or more devoid of 'human' interest. The shape of the station roof and the atmospheric mingling of steam and cloud are the aspects that most absorb him, though the scene is completely urban and modern. It is almost Turner's* Rain, Steam and Speed *brought up to date, in closer focus and minus the rain and the speed.* ❜

35 PIERRE-AUGUSTE RENOIR (1841-1915)
The Seine at Asnières ('La Yole') (6478)

Canvas 0.710 x 0.920 (28 x 36⅛)
Signed, bottom left: Renoir
Purchased, 1982.

The painting represents a site north-west of Paris where the Asnières railway bridge crosses the Seine. Both Van Gogh and Bernard painted at Asnières in the 1880s and the same bridge appears in the background of Seurat's *Bathers, Asnières* (National Gallery No. 3908). The railway bridge linked the port of Clichy, dominated by docks and smoking factories, with the more fashionable suburban area of Asnières. Renoir's painting probably depicts the view looking towards one of the fashionable villas on the Asnières side of the river, a vista which excludes the harsher industrial aspects of the site.

The artist presents us with an idyllic scene of Parisians at leisure. During the 1870s Asnières was a popular resort for boating and, situated only four kilometres from the Gare St. Lazare, it was readily accessible to the Parisian public.

Renoir painted a number of paintings of the river with rowers in the late 1870s and early 1880s and Douglas Cooper has proposed a date of 1879 for this picture. As the *Canotiers à Chatou*, (National Gallery of Art, Washington), which is more strident in colour and looser in handling, is dated 1879, *The Seine at Asnières* may be slightly earlier.

The Seine at Asnières is comparable to several other Impressionist paintings of boating on the Seine. The motif of the steam train crossing the bridge, for example, appears in many of Monet's paintings of the 1870s. Renoir's friend, Gustave Caillebotte, had also painted scenes of rowing on the Seine which he showed at the 1879 Impressionist exhibition. In Caillebotte's works, however, the depiction of rowing as a sport is in marked contrast to the pleasurable and leisurely activity enjoyed by the young ladies in Renoir's painting.

The painting belonged first to Victor Chocquet. It was sold at his death in 1899 to the dealer, Bernheim Jeune, and in 1929 it was bought by Samuel Courtauld. The National Gallery purchased the painting in 1982.

The Seine at Asnières was recently exhibited at the 1985/86 Renoir exhibition at the Hayward Gallery, London, the Galeries Nationales du Grand Palais, Paris, and the Museum of Fine Arts, Boston. The results of a scientific examination of the palette used by Renoir for this painting are discussed in an article by Ashok Roy, 'The Palettes of Three Impressionist Paintings', in the *National Gallery Technical Bulletin*, vol. 9, 1985.

' Of all the Impressionists Renoir is the hardest to assess fairly, so variable is the quality of his work — as indeed the Gallery's few paintings by him demonstrate. Hedonism as resolute as his runs the risk of lapsing into slackness and brainlessness. Hedonistic as is the mood of this painting, it nevertheless carefully captures the almost noisy effect of sunlight striking water. The river — not the sky — is the main motif and source of the sense of intense brilliance which is conveyed. Heat and light on a sunny summer's day in the country exude from it as powerfully as does the wintry atmosphere of an urban scene from Monet's Gare St-Lazare. '

---

36 ODILON REDON (1840-1916)
Ophelia among the Flowers (6438)
Signed, bottom right: ODILON REDON
Pastel, 0.640 x 0.910 (25½ x 37⅞)
Purchased, 1977.

This, the first work by Redon to enter the National Gallery, is one of the very few in British collections. The artist remained unknown until after 1880 when he was acclaimed by the literary *avant-garde* as a leading representative of the Symbolist Movement in France. He was born in Bordeaux and, except for a brief period in the studio of Jean-Léon Gérome, received an informal training from the obscure provincial painter, Stanislas Gorin de Beaux and the graphic artist, Rodolphe Bresdin. Until the 1890s the greater part of Redon's output consisted of charcoal drawings and series of lithographs. His first album, *Dans le rêve*, appeared in 1879, the last, *The Revelation of S. John*, in 1899.

This pastel dates from about 1905-8, after the artist had abandoned black and white work for richly coloured pastels and oil paintings. In this transition to colour Redon was influenced by the work of younger French artists such as Gauguin, Emile Bernard and Maurice Denis. The pastel is one of a group of pictures in which figures and flowers are combined. Shakespearian subjects are uncommon, although Redon draws not infrequently upon such modern writers as Baudelaire, Flaubert and Edgar Allan Poe, and upon ancient mythology. Flowers become central to his art after the turn of the century, and it seems that initially this picture showed a vase of flowers on a table. Subsequently Redon turned the drawing on its side and added a profile and landscape background.

The pastel has been included in several exhibitions including the 1961/62 Odilon Redon, Gustave

Moreau and Rodolphe Bresdin exhibition held at the Museum of Modern Art, New York, and the Art Institute of Chicago.

The pastel was formerly in the Albert D. Lasker Collection, U.S.A., and was purchased, with the aid of the National Art-Collections Fund, from Marlborough Fine Art Ltd in 1977.

It is included in the summary catalogue of the artist's work by Klaus Berger, *Odilon Redon, Fantasy and Colour*, 1964.

' Redon was an exact contemporary of Monet's, though one might not guess it, and this fiercely glowing pastel, if less overtly fantastic and dreamlike than some of Redon's other work, reminds us that there were keen artistic sensibilities alive concerned with an interior, subjective world far away from that of the Impressionists. In that alone, it is a useful acquisition — and a welcome one. '

37   GUSTAV KLIMT (1862-1918)
Hermine Gallia, 1904   (6434)
Canvas, 1.705 x 0.965 (67 x 38)
Inscribed, in a *cartouche* upper right: *Gustav Klimt 1904*
Purchased, 1976.

The sitter was born Hermine Hamburger on 14 July 1870 in Freudenthal (Silesia); she died on 16 February 1936. The daughter of a brewer, in 1893 she married her uncle, Moriz Gallia, who bore the title *Regierungsrat* received in recognition of his donation of a large and important painting by Giovanni Segantini to the recently founded Austrian state collection of modern art. Moriz Gallia commissioned from Baron Kraus, a leading Viennese architect, his house at Wohllebengasse 4, where the decoration of the first-floor apartment was designed by Josef Hoffmann. In this Wiener Werkstätte interior Hermine Gallia's portrait took its place with another painting by Klimt, *A Beech Forest*, now lost.

Moriz Gallia's commission of this portrait must have been given around 1902 or 1903, the years when Klimt was undergoing attacks from the professorial body of the University on account of his painting, *Philosophy*, designed as one of a series of three to decorate the ceiling of the main hall there. Moriz Gallia was clearly a supporter of Klimt at a time when support was most needed. The date on the portrait indicates the year of completion, for it was shown, in an unfinished although well-advanced state, in the Klimt-Kollektive exhibition at the Secession in November/December 1903.

More than thirty-seven preparatory sketches have been related to the portrait. No chronology can be applied to them. Some show Hermine seated in profile, others full face. In others she is shown with the costume props which were part of the studio collection — the muff and boa and so on. Klimt's interest in the personality of his sitters was limited, and his drawings betray this in a fundamental way, for the faces are often wholly void save for the faintest mask-like traces. His drawings, invariably made in pencil on cheap buff-coloured paper, show him re-organizing the pose, experimenting with the sinuous rhythms of the drapery. In the case of Hermine Gallia, it is the drapery which is the determining feature of the final painting. It floats around the upper torso.

Costume was of great importance to Klimt. If a sitter did not already own a suitable Wiener Werkstätte dress, then one had to be made, by the Flöge sisters, one of whom was Klimt's common law wife.

Chronologically and stylistically, the portrait belongs to one of a group which was to end in 1905 when Klimt adopted his well-known 'Byzantine' style. A suggestion of the mosaic treatment is visible in the portrait of Hermine, for the carpet makes overt reference to the kind of mosaic work which had so impressed the artist when he visited Ravenna for the first time in early 1903. By that time Josef Hoffmann had already used mosaic-like patterns and this may also have been an influence.

For a full account of the painting see *Vienna 1913*, catalogue to the exhibition in Melbourne 1984, with an essay on the portrait by Alistair Smith.

The painting was sold by members of the Gallia family at Christie's on 30 November 1971, and was acquired by the Gallery in 1976 from a foreign owner via Fischer Fine Art Ltd, with the help of a donation from a group of anonymous benefactors.

❛ Only gradually is the full story of Western art towards the end of the 19th century and beginning of this century becoming told. In concise histories of art, Vienna tends to be passed over briefly, if mentioned at all. Yet Klimt and Schiele were two outstanding artists of the period. Klimt himself had several styles, and this portrait shows only one of them. It is intensely personal and individual, at once evanescent and haunting, the portrait, it must be said, of a dress as much as of the wearer. ❜

---

38   HENRI MATISSE (1869-1954)
Portrait of Greta Moll   (6450)

Signed bottom left: Henri Matisse 1908
Canvas, 0.930 x 0.735 (36¼ x 29)
Purchased, 1979.

The sitter, Margarete Moll, born in Mulhouse in 1884, was a sculptress and painter. Like her husband, the German painter, Oskar Moll, she was a pupil, for a time, of Matisse, and an early collector of his works. In her account of the execution of her portrait (published in *Matisse: His Art and his Public* by Alfred H. Barr) she tells how she sat ten times for the artist early in 1908. The blouse was at one time lavender-white and the skirt green. Finally, apparently influenced by a Veronese female portrait in the Louvre, Matisse broadened the arms and gave stronger emphasis to her features.

The *Greta Moll* is the first work by Matisse to enter the Collection and is rare in his oeuvre in being a commissioned portrait. Nevertheless, while the head is more firmly modelled than in other paintings of this period, the flat, linear design is characteristic and indicates the importance of the work of Gauguin and other Post-Impressionists in his early development. The flowered cotton print, against which Greta Moll is placed, reappears in a number of other works of these years, including the famous *Harmony in Red* (originally *Harmony in Blue*) which like many of Matisse's early masterpieces was bought by the Russian, Sergei Shchukin, and is now in the Hermitage, Leningrad.

For long in the sitter's possession, the portrait of Greta Moll later passed into private collections in Texas and Switzerland. It has been exhibited often, firstly in Berlin by Cassirer in 1908-9. It figured in the important Matisse show at the Museum of Modern Art, New York in 1931, and at the Pompidou Centre, Paris, in the 1978 Paris/Berlin exhibition.

The painting was shown most recently in the 1982/83 Matisse exhibition at the Kunsthalle, Düsseldorf, and the Kunsthaus, Zurich.

❛ There need be no argument about Matisse fitting into a Collection preponderantly of 'old Masters'. With Braque, he is the most classic of modern artists, illustrating and asserting the power of pure line and the beauty of pure colour, in a way that carries one back to the beginnings of Italian painting, to Duccio and Ugolino. Yet this portrait breaks many of the conventions that had grown up in Western painting by the 19th century. It challenges us to keep looking at art with fresh eyes and the fewest possible prejudices — and in that it has its message for every visitor to the Gallery. ❜

Acquisitions not included in the exhibition

6425   Rachel Ruysch (1664-1750)
Flowers in a Vase
Canvas, 0.570 x 0.435 (22½ x 17⅛)
Bequeathed by Alan Evans, 1974

6426   Jean-Joseph Taillasson (1745-1809)
Virgil reading the Aeneid to Augustus and Octavia
Canvas, 1.472 x 1.669 (57⅞ x 65¾)
Purchased, 1974.

6428   Hyacinthe Rigaud (1659-1743)
Portrait of Antoine Paris
Canvas, 1.447 x 1.105 (59 x 43½)
Purchased, 1975

6436   Gustave Moreau (1826-98)
S. George and the Dragon
Canvas, 1.410 x 0.965 (55½ x 38)
Purchased, 1976

6437   Anthony van Dyck (1599-1641)
Lady Elizabeth Thimbleby and Dorothy, Viscountess Andover
Canvas, 1.321 x 1.490 (52 x 59)
Purchased by private treaty from Earl Spencer, 1977

6439   Jean-Baptiste-Camille Corot (1796-1875)
Peasants under the Trees at Dawn
Canvas, 0.282 x 0.397 (11⅛ x 15⅝)
Purchased, 1977

6443   Cornelis van Haarlem (1562-1638)
The Preaching of S. John the Baptist
Canvas, 1.000 x 1.800 (39⅓ x 70¾)
Purchased, 1978

6444   Willem Kalf (1619-93)
Still-life with the drinking-horn of the S. Sebastian Archers' Guild, a lobster and glasses
Canvas, 0.864 x 1.022 (34 x 40¼)
Bequeathed by R.S. Newall, 1978

6446   Carlo Saraceni (1589-1620)
Jacob reproaching Laban for giving him Leah in place of Rachel
Copper, 0.285 x 0.353 (11⅛ x 13⅞)
Bequeathed by Benedict Nicolson, 1978

6447   Jean-François Millet (1814-75)
The Winnower
Canvas, 1.005 x 0.710 (39½ x 28)
Purchased, with the aid of anonymous benefactors, 1978

6449   Pablo Picasso (1881-1973)
Fruit dish, bottle and guitar
Canvas, 0.920 x 0.730 (36¼ x 28¾)
Purchased, 1979

6453   Pontormo (1494-1557)
Joseph's brothers beg for help
Panel, 0.363 x 1.425 (14⁵⁄₁₆ x 56⅛)
Purchased, together with Nos. 6451 and 6452, by private treaty with a contribution from the NACF (Eugene Cremetti Fund), 1979

6454   Jean-François Detroy (1679-1752)
Time unveiling Truth
Canvas, 2.030 x 2.080 (80 x 82)
Purchased by private treaty from the estate of Dr E.I. Schapiro, 1979

6455   Italian School, 17th century
S. John the Baptist
Canvas, 0.778 x 0.623 (30⅝ x 24½)
Bequeathed by Dame Joan Evans, 1979

6456   Claude-Oscar Monet (1840-1926)
Bathers at La Grenouillère
Canvas, 0.730 x 0.920 (28¾ x 36¼)
Bequeathed by Richard and Sophie Walzer, 1979

6457   Paul Cézanne (1839-1906)
Landscape with Poplars
Canvas, 0.710 x 0.580 (28 x 22¾)
Bequeathed by Richard and Sophie Walzer, 1979

6459   Pompeo Girolamo Batoni (1708-87)
Portrait of a Gentleman
Canvas, 134.6 x 96.5 (53 x 38)
Purchased, 1980

6460   Jacob Pynas (c.1585-after 1656)
Landscape with Narcissus
Panel, 0.476 x 0.628 (18¾ x 24¾)
Presented in memory of Keith Roberts, 1980

6462   Jan Baptist Weenix (1621-c.1663)
An Italian Courtyard
Canvas, 0.845 x 0.685 (33¼ x 27)
Purchased, 1980

6464   Jan van Goyen (1596-1656)
The Mouth of a River
Panel, 0.332 x 0.476 (13 x 18¾)
Gift of Mrs Alice Bleecker, 1981

6465 Willem van de Velde (1633-1707)
Ships in a Calm
Panel, 0.357 x 0.433 (14 x 17)
Gift of Mrs Alice Bleecker, 1981

6466 Jean-Baptiste-Camille Corot (1796-1875)
The Oak in the Valley
Canvas, 0.400 x 0.530 (15¾ x 20¾)
Gift of Mrs Alice Bleecker, 1981

6467 Jean-Baptiste-Camille Corot (1796-1875)
Souvenir de Palluel
Canvas, 0.270 x 0.350 (10½ x 13¾)
Gift of Mrs Alice Bleecker, 1981

6468 Jean-Louis-Ernest Meissonier (1815-91)
A Man in Black smoking a Pipe
Oak, 0.324 x 0.235 (12¾ x 9¼)
Gift of Mrs Alice Bleecker, 1981

6470 Master of the St. Bartholomew Altarpiece
(active c.1470-c.1510)
The Deposition of Christ from the Cross
Oak, 0.749 x 0.473 (29½ x 18¾)
Purchased by private treaty, 1981

6472 Willem Koekkoek (1839-95)
A View of Oudewater
Canvas, 0.844 x 0.648 (33¼ x 25½)
Bequeathed by Miss J.M. Hawkins Turner,
1982

6473 Joseph Parrocel (1646 - 1704)
*The Boar Hunt: an allegory of the Continent
of Europe*
Canvas, 1.105 x 1.060 (43½ x 41¾)
Purchased, 1982

6474 Joseph Parrocel (1646 - 1704)
*The Hawking Party: an allegory of the
Continent of Asia*
Canvas, 1.105 x 1.060 (43½ x 41¾)
Purchased, 1982

6475 Hans von Aachen (c.1552-1615)
The Amazement of the Gods
Copper, 0.360 x 0.465 (14¼ x 18¼)
Purchased 1982

6476 Moses van Uyttenbroeck (before 1600-47)
Landscape with Mythological Figures
Panel, 0.559 x 0.770 (22 x 23)
Purchased 1982

6477 Nicolas Poussin (1595?-1655)
The Triumph of Pan
Canvas, 1.340 x 1.450 (52¾ x 57)
Purchased with contributions from the
National Heritage Memorial Fund and the
NACF, 1982

6482 Sir William Boxall (1800-79)
Self Portrait
Canvas, 0.530 x 0.416 (20¾ x 16⅜)
Presented by Mr Christopher Wood, 1983

6483 Hendrick Ter Brugghen (1588?-1629)
The Concert
Canvas, 0.991 x 1.168 (39 x 45⅞)
Purchased with a contribution from the
National Heritage Memorial Fund and
donations from the NA-CF and the Pilgrim
Trust, 1983

6485-6 Ugolino di Nerio (active 1317-27)
David; Two Angels
Poplar, 0.550 x 0.315 (21⅝ x 12⅜) and
0.270 x 0.560 (10½ x 22)
Purchased by private treaty, 1983

6487 Luca Giordano (1634-1705)
*Perseus turning Phineas and his followers to
stone*
Canvas, 2.850 x 3.660 (168½ x 172)
Purchased, 1983

6488 Edouard Vuillard (1868-1940)
Madame André Wormser and her Children
Canvas, 0.890 x 1.165 (35 x 45⅝)
Presented by M. Olivier Wormser, 1983

6491 Salvator Rosa (1615-73)
Witches at their Incantations
Canvas, 0.740 x 1.345 (29 x 53)
Purchased, 1984

6494 Anthony van Dyck (1599-1641)
Charity
Panel, 1.482 x 1.075 (58⅝ x 42¼)
Purchased by private treaty, 1984

6497 Attributed to the Master of the
St. Bartholomew Altarpiece (active c.1470-
1510)
Triptych: *The Virgin and Child with Musical
Angels*
Exterior: *The Annunciation*
Oak, 0.520 x 0.380 (19½ x 15), round top
Purchased, 1984

6500 Jean-Baptiste Greuze (1725-1805)
Portrait of a Man
Canvas, 0.640 x 0.540 (25 x 21)
Purchased 1985

6501 Francisco Bayeu y Subias (1734-95)
*The Vision of the Madonna of the Pillar to
St. James*
Canvas, 0.530 x 0.840 (20⅞ x 33⅛)
Purchased, 1985

Sir Michael Levey: bibliography of principal writings on the visual arts

BOOKS and PAMPHLETS

The Eighteenth-Century Italian Schools,
National Gallery Catalogues, London, 1956

Six Great Painters: Michelangelo, Titian, Rubens, Rembrandt, Gainsborough, Van Gogh,
London, 1956

A Brief History of the National Gallery,
London, 1957

Twenty-four Masterpieces from the National Gallery,
London, 1958.

Painting in Eighteenth-Century Venice,
London, 1959

A Second Book of Twenty-four Masterpieces from the National Gallery
London, 1959

The German School,
National Gallery Catalogues, London, 1959

A Concise History of Painting from Giotto to Cézanne,
London, 1962

Canaletto Paintings in the Collection of Her Majesty the Queen,
London, 1964

Dürer,
London, 1964

The Later Italian Pictures in the Collection of Her Majesty the Queen,
London, 1964

A Room-to-Room guide to the National Gallery,
National Gallery, London, 1964

Rococo to Revolution, Major Trends in Eighteenth Century Painting,
London, 1966

Tiepolo: Banquet of Cleopatra, (Charlton Lecture)
Newcastle University, 1966

Bronzino,
London, 1967

Early Renaissance,
Harmondsworth, 1967

A History of Western Art,
London, 1968

Canaletto and some Venetian Festivals,
National Gallery, London, 1968

Holbein's 'Christina of Denmark, Duchess of Milan',
National Gallery, London, 1968

'Marriage à la Mode' by William Hogarth,
National Gallery, London, 1970

Painting at Court,
(Wrightsman Lectures 1968)
London, 1971

The Complete Paintings of Botticelli (Introduction),
London, 1970

The Seventeenth- and Eighteenth-Century Italian Schools,
National Gallery Catalogues, London, 1971

The Nude,
(Themes and Painters in the National Gallery No. 1)
National Gallery, London, 1972

Art and Architecture of the Eighteenth-Century in France (with W. Kalnein), Harmondsworth, 1972.

The Venetian Scene
(Themes and Painters in the National Gallery No. 6)
National Gallery, London, 1973

Botticelli,
(Themes and Painters in the National Gallery No. 11)
National Gallery, London, 1974

The World of Ottoman Art,
London, 1975

Gainsborough: The Painter's Daughters chasing a Butterfly,
Painting in Focus No. 4
National Gallery, London, 1975

High Renaissance,
Harmondsworth, 1975

A Royal Subject: Portraits of Queen Charlotte,
National Gallery Exhibtion Catalogue, London 1977

Ruisdael: Jacob van Ruisdael and other painters of his family,
(Themes and Painters in the National Gallery Series, No. 7)
National Gallery, London, 1977

Velázquez and Murillo,
National Gallery Slide Books, London, 1978

The Case of Walter Pater,
London, 1978

Sir Thomas Lawrence,
National Portrait Gallery, Exhibition catalogue,
London, 1979

The Painter Depicted. Painters as a subject in painting,
London, 1981

The Neglected National Gallery. An exhibition of paintings from the Lower Floor,
National Gallery, London, 1983

Giovanni Battista Tiepolo,
London, 1986

ARTICLES and ESSAYS

1953   'Canaletto's Regatta Paintings'
Burlington Magazine, XCV, November 1953,
pp. 365-6.

1954   'Two organ doors from S. Bartolommeo at Vicenza'
Burlington Magazine, XCVI, June 1954,
pp.178-181.

1955   'Tiepolo's *Banquet of Cleopatra* at Melbourne'
Arte Veneta, IX, 1955, pp.199-203.

'A Sketch by Corrado Giaquinto'
Burlington Magazine, XCVII, January 1955, p. 19.

'Tiepolo's Altar-piece for San Salvatore at Venice'
Burlington Magazine, XCVII, April 1955,
pp.116-120

'The National Gallery Acquisitions since the War'
Studio, CXLIX, March 1955, pp.65-75

1956   'A Sketch by Zompini for the Scuola dei Carmini'
Arte Veneta, X, 1956, pp.207-208

1957   'Panini, St Peter's and Cardinal de Polignac'
Burlington Magazine, XCIX, January 1957,
pp.53-54

'Tiepolo's *Empire of Flora*'
Burlington Magazine, XCIX, March 1957,
pp.88-91

'The Modello for Tiepolo's Altar-piece at Nymphenberg'
Burlington Magazine, XCIX, August 1957,
pp.256-258

'Tiepolo's treatment of classical story at Villa Valmarana'
Journal of the Warburg and Courtauld Institutes, XX, July-December 1957, pp. 298-317.

1958   'Art Exhibitions in 18th century Venice' (with F. Haskell)
Arte Veneta, XII, 1958, pp.179-184

'A Note on Marshal Schulenburg's Collection'
Arte Veneta, XII, 1958, p. 221

'Reconstruction of a Westphalian Altar-piece: the Herzebrock Altar'
Burlington magazine, C, August 1958, pp.304-306

'Painters and Painting at the *Age of Rococo* exhibition in Munich' (with F. Haskell)
Burlington Magazine, C, December 1958,
p.422-427

'Some Paintings by Dietrich for J-G Wille'
Gazette des Beaux-Arts, 6th Per., LI, January 1958, pp.33-40

1959   'Francesco Zuccarelli in England'
Italian Studies, XIV, 1959, pp.

'French and Italian Pictures at Waddesdon'
Gazette des Beaux-Arts, LIV, July-August 1959,
pp.57-66

'Wilson and Zuccarelli at Venice'
Burlington Magazine, CI, April 1959, pp.139-143

1960   'Tiepolo and his Age'
Art and Ideas in Eighteenth Century Italy,
Rome 1960, pp.94-113

'An Early Dated Veronese and Veronese's Early Work'
Burlington Magazine, CII, March 1960,
pp.107-111.

'Two Paintings by Tiepolo from the Algarotti Collection'
Burlington Magazine, CII, June 1960, pp.250-257

'An English Commission to Guardi'
Burlington Magazine, CII, August 1960,
pp.365-366

'Botticelli and 19th century England
Journal of the Warburg & Courtauld Institutes, XXIII, 1960, pp.291-306

1961   'The Real Theme of Watteau's *Embarkation for Cythera*'
Burlington Magazine, CIII, May 1961, pp.180-185

'Domenico Tiepolo's earliest frescoes at Zianigo: a Revised Date'
Burlington Magazine, CIII, August 1961,
pp.355-356

'Minor aspects of Dürer's interest in Venetian Art'
Burlington Magazine, CIII, December 1961,
pp.510-513

1962 'Notes on the Royal Collection II, Artemisia Gentileschi's *Self Portrait* at Hampton Court' *Burlington Magazine*, CIV, February 1962, pp.79-81.

'Two Footnotes to any Tiepolo Monograph' *Burlington Magazine*, CIV, March 1962, pp.118-119

'A Prince of Court Painters: Bronzino' *Apollo*, LXXVI, May 1962, pp.165-172

'Canaletto's fourteen paintings and Visentini's *Prospectus Magni Canalis*' *Burlington Magazine*, CIV, August 1962, pp.333-341

'Charles I and Baglione' *Burlington Magazine*, CIV, August 1962, pp.344-347

'Sebastiano Ricci's *Heads* after Veronese' *Burlington Magazine*, CIV, August 1962, p. 351

'Marco Ricci and *Madama Smit Burlington Magazine*, CIV, August 1962, pp.351-352

'A Claude Signature and Date revealed after Cleaning' *Burlington Magazine*, CIV, September 1962, pp.390-391

'Raphael Revisited' *Apollo*, LXXVI, November 1962, pp.678-683

'Eine Altartafel aus der Werkstatt des Meisters von Liesborn' *Westfalen. Hefte für Geschichte, Kunst und Volkskunde* 40, Band 1962, Heft 3

1963 'France and Italy: Artistic Contacts in the Eighteenth Century' *Apollo*, LXXVII, March 1963, pp.177-181

'Poussin's *Neptune and Amphitrite* at Philadelphia: a re-identification rejected' *Journal of the Warburg & Courtauld Institutes*, XXVI, 1963, pp.359-360

'A Loan of 18th c. Venetian Drawings to America' *Art International*, VIII

'British Painting in the Sixties' *London Magazine*, August 1963

1964 'Modern? Art?' *London Magazine*, January 1964

'Reason and Passion in Jacques-Louis David' *Apollo*, LXXX, September 1964, pp.206-211

'A Watteau rediscovered: *Le Printemps* for Crozat' *Burlington Magazine*, CVI, February 1964, pp.53-59

'The Pose of Pigalle's *Mercury*' *Burlington Magazine*, CVI, October 1964, p.462

1965 'Tintoretto and the theme of Miraculous Intervention' (The Selwyn Brinton Lecture) *Journal of the Royal Society of Arts*, August, 1965

'A New Identity for Saly's *Bust of a Young Girl*' *Burlington Magazine*, CVII, February 1965, p.91

'Egon Schiele' *The Lugano Review*, March 1965

1966 'Die Mitteltafel des Liesborner Hochaltars in neuem Licht' *Westfalen. Hefte Für Geschichte, Kunst und Volkskunde* 1966

'Raphael Restored' *Sunday Times Magazine*, 13 March 1986

1967 'The Relationship between national and provincial art galleries' *Museums Journal*, 1967, pp.120-124

'A Hothouse called Ingres' *Sunday Times Magazine*, 15 January 1967

'Sacred and Profane Significance in two paintings by Bronzino' *Studies in Renaissance and Baroque Art* presented to Anthony Blunt on his 60th birthday, London 1967

1968 'Looking for Quality in Pictures' *British Journal of Aesthetics*, VIII, January 1968, pp.3-15

'Three New Galleries' *Architectural Design*, October 1968

1969 'Lord Leighton's Trouble' *Sunday Times Magazine*, 2 November 1969

1970 'Blest Pair of Sirens, Boucher and Tiepolo' *Sunday Times Magazine*, 6 December 1970

1971 'Dürer and England' *Anzeiger Germanischen Nationalmuseums*, 1971/2, pp.157-164

'The Ducal Palace at Urbino' *Sunday Times Magazine*, 21 March 1971

1972 'To Honour Albrecht Dürer: some 1971 Manifestations' *Burlington Magazine*, CXIV, February 1972, pp.63-71

'A painter most speedy: Cranach'
Sunday Times magazine, 17 December 1972

1973 *Dürer and the Renaissance*
in C. Dodwell (Ed.) *Essays on Dürer*
Manchester 1973

'Solimena's *Dido receiving Aeneas and Cupid disguised as Ascanius*'
Burlington Magazine, CXV, June 1973,
pp.385-390

1974 'The revolutionary manifesto of Jan van Eyck'
Observer Magazine, 22 September 1974

1975 'London's National Gallery is 150 years old'
Art Gallery, 10, 1975

'Lawrence's "Portrait of Pope Pius VII"'
Burlington Magazine, CXVII, April 1975,
pp.194-204

'Sir Martin Davies'
Burlington Magazine, CXVII, November 1975,
pp.729-731

'A Little-Known Director: Sir William Boxall'
Apollo, CI, May 1975, pp.354-359

1976 'My Wonders of the World'
Sunday Times Magazine, 9 October 1977

'Putting the art back into art history'
Leonardo, IX, no. 1, 1976, pp.63-65

1980 'Three slight revisions to Tiepolo scholarship'
Arte Veneta, XXXII, 1980, pp.418-422

1982 'A Boucher Mythological Painting Interpreted'
Burlington Magazine, CXXIV, July 1982,
pp.442-446

1984 'The ambiguous art of Tissot'
Antique Collector, June 1984, pp.80-87

1986 'Neglected Norway'
Antique Collector, July 1986

'French Acquisitions of Recent Years at the National Gallery'
Apollo, CXXIII, June 1986, pp.378-85

'The Earliest Years of the Burlington: a brief retrospect'
Burlington Magazine, CXXVII, July 1986,
pp. 474-477

PRINCIPAL REVIEWS

1957 'The Bernardo Bellotto exhibition at Whitechapel'
Burlington Magazine, XCIX, June 1957,
pp.206-207

1960 'Count Seilern's Italian Pictures and Drawings'
Burlington Magazine, CII, March 1960,
pp.122-123

1961 'The German Exhibition at Manchester' (with C. White)
Burlington Magazine, CIII, December 1961,
pp.485-490

'The Eighteenth-Century Italian Painting Exhibition at Paris: Some Corrections and Suggestions'
Burlington Magazine, CIII, April 1961,
pp.139-143

1962 'A Morassi: A complete catalogue of the Paintings of G.B. Tiepolo'
Art Bulletin, XLV, 1962, pp.293-295

1963 'Domenico Tiepolo: his earliest activity and a monograph'
Burlington Magazine, CV, March 1963,
pp.128-129.

1966 'F.J. Sanchez Canton: Goya and the black paintings'
Museums Journal, 1966, pp.67-68

'The Life and Work of Houdon' by Louis Réau
Burlington Magazine, CVIII, March 1966,
p.147-148

1968 'Ingres at Cambridge and Paris'
Master Drawings, VI, no. 1 1968, pp.44-47

1969 'Ingres for Ingres' Sake': Review of Ingres, R. Rosenblum, London 1967
Art News, April 1969

'Pignatti T.: Longhi', London 1969
Art Bulletin, LII, pp.463-464

1970 'Eberhard Ruhmer: Grünewald Drawings', London 1970
Master Drawings, 9, p.62-63

'Otto Benesch: German Painting from Dürer to Holbein'
Burlington Magazine, CXII, March 1970,
pp.179-183

'The Order of St John in Malta exhibition at Valletta'
Burlington Magazine, CXII, August 1970,
p.554-557

1971 'T. Hodgkinson: The James A. de Rothschild Collection at Waddesdon Manor: Sculpture'
Burlington Magazine, CXIII, March 1971,
pp.162-165

'The Dürer Exhibition at Nuremberg' (with C. White)
Burlington Magazine, CXIII, August 1971,
pp.484-488

'Boucher, Gravures et Dessins'
Master Drawings, IX, no. 3, pp.280-281

1973   'Bernardo Bollotto, by Stefan Kosakiewics'
Burlington Magazine, CXV, September 1973,
pp.615-616

1977   'Jean-Baptiste Greuze (1725−1805)'
Master Drawings, XV, 1977, No. 3,
pp.280−282

'W.G. Constable, Canaletto, Oxford, 1977'
Burlington Magazine, CXIX, December 1977,
p.866

'Tulips, Arabesques and Turbans at Leighton
House'
Burlington Magazine, CXXIV, July 1982,
pp.466-469

'Van Dyck in England at the National Portrait
Gallery'
Burlington Magazine, CXXV, February 1983,
p.106, pp.109−110

1978   'Lise Duclaux, Musée du Louvre, Inventaire
général des Dessins. Ecole Française, XII,
Nadar−Ozanne, French Landscape Drawings
and Sketches of the Eighteenth Century.'
Master Drawings, XVI, no. 3, pp.307−311.

1981   François Souchal, French Sculptors of the 17th
and 18th Centuries. The Reign of Louis XIV,
Vol. II, *Burlington Magazine*, CXXIII,
December 1981, pp.751−752

1984   Ileana Chiappini di Sorio, 'Palazzo Pisani
Moretta',
Burlington Magazine, CXXVI, August 1984,
p.509.

1985   M. Roland Michel, 'Lajoue et l'Art Rocaille',
Burlington Magazine, CXXVII, April 1985,
pp.236−237.

National Gallery
Director's choice: selected acquisitions
1973-1986.
1. National Gallery − Catalogs
I. Title   II. Levey, Michael
750′. 74′02132   N1070

ISBN 0-947645-14-4

Exhibition designed by Sally McIntosh, National Gallery Design Studio
Catalogue designed by Simon Loxley
Printed by Balding + Mansell Limited, London and Wisbech